The Home Book of
Jewish Cookery

THE HOME BOOK OF
Jewish Cookery

❖❖❖❖❖

Judy Jackson

FABER AND FABER
London · Boston

First published in 1981
by Faber and Faber Limited
3 Queen Square London WC1N 3AU
Filmset in Monophoto by
Latimer Trend & Company Ltd Plymouth
Printed in Great Britain by
Redwood Burn Ltd Trowbridge and Esher
All rights reserved

British Library Cataloguing in Publication Data

Jackson, Judy
The Home Book of Jewish Cookery
1. Cookery, Jewish
I. Title
641.5'676   TX724
ISBN 0-571-11697-3
ISBN 0-571-11737-6 Pbk

FOR MICHAEL
AND FOR DANIEL, TIMOTHY AND DAVID

Contents

Introduction

Jewish cookery is more than a collection of recipes handed down from our grandparents. Traditional food is a part of the history of the Jewish people. It reflects the hard times, the wanderings, the memories and the joys of a very mixed race. What we eat in our homes today is based on the foods of the countries where Jews made their homes. 'Typical' Jewish food is as varied as any international menu. The Ashkenazi Jews (from Russia, Poland, Germany and Eastern Europe) specialize in borscht (beetroot soup), knaidlach (soup dumplings), rye bread and paper-thin strudel pastry. The Sephardi Jews (from Spain, Portugal and the Middle East) prefer stuffed aubergine and rice dishes, and sweet almond desserts. What all Jewish dishes have in common is that everything we eat conforms to the strict laws of Orthodox Judaism (see pp. 15–19 for a more detailed explanation); maybe because certain restrictions have been imposed upon us, we have become even more inventive in adapting the foods of the countries we live in to our own way of life.

However, life today is very different in style from the way our parents and grandparents lived. They could spend two whole days preparing for Shabbat (Sabbath, Saturday), and this involved kneading the dough for the plaited challa, chopping fish by hand and stretching and rolling the strudel pastry. Few people today are prepared to spend so much time in the kitchen, but since the preparation of food is so bound up with the happy occasions which make up the Jewish year, most of us are very reluctant to give up serving the dishes which are so greatly appreciated by our families and friends. The world is full of jokes about Jewish mothers forcing food on their unwilling children, but there is a lot of truth in the deep-rooted urge to bring the family together in the happy atmosphere of eating and drinking.

Ideally, one should be able to set aside a few 'cooking days', but the problem nowadays seems to be to find the time to devote to cooking. I don't believe the answer lies in the use of substitutes and convenience foods. Certainly, there are many acceptable products on the market—ready-made pasta, pastry, ice cream and tinned and frozen vegetables. But if you have the time to make a meal using fresh produce and what I call 'real' ingredients, the results will be quite different. Where you can save time is by using all the modern equipment you can afford, like mixers, blenders, non-stick pans and time-controlled ovens. However, the biggest time-saver of all is the freezer. If you are lucky enough to own one you can cook when you feel like it and not just before a dinner party or festival; you can make twice the quantity and prepare for the unexpected guest in the same time as it takes you to make an evening meal. Best of all, you can stock your freezer with home-made rolls, danish pastries, crisp biscuits, puréed fruits, meringues, soup stocks, flan cases—the possibilities are endless. You are probably thinking that this sounds like a lot of work in itself, but if you enjoy cooking and can do it in a relaxed atmosphere when you are not rushed, it will save you time when you are tired or busy, and the result will be that you will have a store full of good things.

You may be wondering where to start. In my selection of Jewish recipes I have not attempted to provide a comprehensive encyclopaedia. I have included many well-known dishes, and I have chosen both Sephardi and Ashkenazi recipes. But my choice is a very personal one. I have been collecting recipes since I married. Many of them were not even written down, but were the results of the hours I spent as a child watching my mother in her kitchen and eating the most delicious soups, rich sauces and light pastries. She is still one of the finest cooks I know, and it is from her that I learned to make some of the traditional dishes as well as the countless gâteaux and desserts at which she excels. I have also tried to adapt many international recipes so that they can be used together with the more traditional fare. Good as they are, the chopped liver, knaidlach, cholent and lockshen pudding are not as popular today as they used to be. This is because we are becoming far more health-conscious, and a diet which is rich in animal fats, eggs, sugar and starch is giving way to one which contains more fresh vegetables, fruit, lightly-sauced fish and grilled meat. So in some cases I have changed the old favourites and adapted them slightly to make them lighter or less sweet. Many of the recipes are not, strictly speaking, Jewish, but are included because the original version can often be suitably adapted for the kosher kitchen.

The book is arranged in sections. The first two include hot and cold starters and soups. These are followed by main courses—fish, light dishes and snacks, meat and poultry—and the vegetables and salads to serve with them. The next four sections on desserts, cakes and gâteaux, biscuits and breads are to be avoided by those on a diet but thoroughly recommended to those who believe that life is enriched by the odd indulgence! Finally, there is the chapter on Passover. This includes many recipes which are traditional festival foods, as well as a list of other recipes in the book which may be served during the Passover week.

Because of the prohibition of eating milk with meat (see p. 15), I have also divided both the chapters and all the recipes into 1) those dishes which contain meat, or meat products, 2) those which contain milk or any dairy product, and 3) those which contain neither and are therefore suitable for any meal, and are called 'parev' or neutral dishes. The abbreviations given are:

m   meat
d   dairy
p   parev

My reason for doing this is to make it easier to choose different courses when planning a complete menu.

In writing this book, my main purpose was to gather together a collection of recipes from my own mixed Sephardi and

Ashkenazi background. I then thought it would be a good idea to make it a bit more explanatory for my non-Jewish friends to whom the whole idea of kosher food is new. Finally, by adding some of the ideas I have developed and adapted in my search for slightly more unusual 'kosher' food, I hope to interest many people who have known about Jewish cooking all their lives.

I hope you will enjoy this collection of recipes. I am sure you will be encouraged to try out the secrets handed down from our ancestors of many countries and perhaps to invent some new ideas of your own which will become part of this growing and changing tradition.

Jewish Laws and Festivals: a brief explanation

✳✳✳

The laws of the Jewish religion are designed as a guide for living and the laws governing what we eat are no exception. They originate in a passage in the Bible (Deut. 14) which reads:

> These are the animals you may eat . . . the ox, the sheep . . . and any animals with a parted hoof . . . you may not eat the camel, the hare . . . and the pig . . . you shall regard as unclean. Of creatures that live in the water you may eat all those that have fins and scales. . . . You may eat all clean birds. . . . You shall not eat anything that has died a natural death. . . . You shall not boil a kid in its mother's milk. For you are a people holy to your God.

In a simplified form this means that cows, sheep, poultry and fish are permitted, while pigs, shellfish, snails, etc. are not. However, in order to conform to the laws of Kashrut (dietary laws) the orthodox Jew may only eat permitted animals or fish killed in a humane and carefully specified way; in the case of meat and poultry all blood must be removed by a process of salting and soaking before cooking; and in addition, any meat food must not be eaten with milk or a milk by-product. In practice, this means buying only kosher meat, preparing it for cooking, and separating meat foods from milk by using different cooking and serving utensils and waiting an appropriate time after a meal containing meat before eating anything containing milk. These rules apply throughout the year and whether one is at home or away.

The prohibition of working on Shabbat, as set down in the Ten Commandments, is extended to cooking, as explained in Exodus 16: 'Tomorrow is a day of sacred rest, a Sabbath holy to the Lord. So bake what you want to bake now. . . .' This has resulted in the devising of many dishes which can be prepared before Shabbat or left to cook untouched overnight. The best-known of these is cholent (see Glossary). The origin of the name is slightly confused—some people think it comes from the French *chaud-lent* ('warm-slow') while others believe it derives from the German *schul-ende* ('synagogue-end').

The prohibitions regarding meat and the fact that Jews often lived in poor communities far from the coast led to the development of many recipes which were designed to supplement small quantities of freshwater fish like carp, and this is why gefilte fish (see Glossary) was a staple food in many European homes. In fact, the word 'gefilte' really means stuffed and was originally the stuffing for a large fish. During times of poverty the actual fish was not served and the stuffing was formed into balls which eventually became a delicacy on their own.

Sabbaths and festivals were always special days in the Jewish calendar. The Hebrew for festival is in fact Yomtov, meaning a 'good day', and all the special dishes were saved for these days. Whereas dark bread would be eaten throughout the week, white bread or challa would be baked specially for Shabbat. Vegetables and dumplings would be eaten as ordinary fare, but chickens and meat and rich pastries would be prepared in celebration of the Holy Days.

Each of the festivals has its special traditions.

Rosh Hashana (New Year)

New Year falls in the autumn and is the time when Jews look back over the past year and look forward to a year of health and good fortune. The challa is baked in a special round form to symbolize the cycle of the year and the festival meal begins with apples and honey to provide a sweet start.

Yom Kippur (Day of Atonement)

New Year is followed ten days later by the most solemn day in the Jewish calendar, the Day of Atonement. On this day Jews pray to God for forgiveness for their sins and they must fast from sunset on the eve to sunset on the day itself. The custom is to prepare for the fast by eating foods which are not heavily spiced or seasoned (since drinking even water is not allowed) and to end the fast with tea and cake, often followed by a varied meal which one is sometimes too tired to eat.

Succot (Tabernacles)

In the same month as the Day of Atonement comes the Feast of Tabernacles. This festival commemorates the biblical period when the Jews spent forty years wandering in the desert on their journey from Egypt to Palestine. They had no permanent homes and lived in 'booths'. For this reason we actually build a temporary structure called a succah and eat our meals in it (and some people actually sleep in it) to remind us of what it must have been like to live under the stars with no proper shelter. At this time we also celebrate the gathering of the harvest, and as a thanksgiving we enjoy all the seasonal fruits, often using the foliage and the fruits themselves to decorate the walls and lattice roof of the succah.

Chanucah (Feast of Dedication)

Chanucah is a minor festival commemorating the re-dedication of the Temple after a group of Jewish partisans succeeded in protecting it from the Greek attempt to desecrate it. Today we burn oil or candles every night for eight nights to commemorate the fact that the small amount of oil found available for kindling the Everlasting Light in the Temple miraculously lasted for eight days. Perhaps this is why the foods associated with Chanucah, like latkes (see Glossary), are often fried in oil.

Purim (Feast of Esther)

Purim is another holiday celebrating a triumph over oppression in Jewish history. Queen Esther managed to foil the plot of the wicked Haman to exterminate the Jews, and today children traditionally have fancy dress parties and eat delicacies called 'Hamantaschen' and 'Oznei Haman' (Haman's ears).

Pesach (Passover)

Passover is the only festival in the calendar when what we eat is entirely symbolic of the origin of the Holy Days. Here again, as with the laws about meat, the commandment to 'keep the Passover to the Lord' (Deut.16) has led to very detailed definition of what we should and should not do. The festival is in commemoration of the time when the Jews (Hebrews) left Egypt where they had been slaves under the Pharaohs, and because they had no time to wait for the bread dough to rise, they were forced to bake it quickly and eat it as unleavened cakes.

Passover falls at around the same time as Easter in the Christian calendar. On the first two nights of the festival we have a Seder service which is a combination of gathering the family together to tell the story and illustrating it by showing and tasting its various symbols. (The Last Supper probably consisted of this meal.) For the following eight days no bread, flour, or anything made from leaven is permitted, and only matzah (see Glossary) and cakes and biscuits made from matzo meal, may be used.

During Passover the word kosher takes on a different meaning and does not only apply to meat. Since the laws about not eating anything leavened are extremely strict, everything bottled, canned or pre-prepared must be done under supervision and this is what 'kosher for Passover' means.

Shavuot (Pentecost)

This is the last of the festivals and means literally 'weeks'. It commemorates the giving of the Ten Commandments on Mount Sinai and comes exactly seven weeks after Passover. The special foods associated with it seem to have the rather tenuous connection that the Jews waited so long on Mount Sinai that their milk soured and turned to cheese, so we celebrate by eating blintzes (see Glossary) and cheesecake. However, the festival itself reminds us that the Jews were redeemed from slavery for a purpose—to live in accordance with the law.

The observance of the laws and festivals is basically a framework for living. A knowledge of the reasons behind them will perhaps explain customs which might seem outdated today. The laws themselves are extremely detailed and I have, of course, only given a brief outline here.

Notes on Ingredients

Jewish cookery does not require a large number of unusual ingredients. The true traditional recipes may be made from items in a basic store cupboard. However, there is a challenge in modern Jewish cooking to adapt recipes which contain combinations or ingredients which are prohibited by the dietary laws. In this area certain substitutes do give an acceptable alternative, so here are a few suggestions, as well as some notes on particularly kosher ingredients.

OILS AND FATS

Butter is most commonly used with dairy or fish recipes.

Oil : corn or olive oil is used as it is parev or neutral. Corn oil is used for deep frying and olive oil is most often used in cooking vegetables like aubergines and in salads.

Margarine containing only vegetable oil and no animal fat is also parev and is therefore often used in biscuits and pastry.

Chicken fat is the most traditional fat used for frying in meat dishes. It is the white or pale yellow fat taken from a chicken, which is then 'rendered down' (or melted slowly), sometimes with a slice of onion, and then strained into pots for use in any meat or poultry dish.

COMMERCIAL PAREV PRODUCTS

Parev whip is a white non-dairy liquid, which, when whipped, gives the consistency (but not the taste) of fresh cream.

Parev milk powder is a powder made from non-dairy ingredients, used with liquids to give a cream flavour.

Parev stock powder is a yellow powder which gives the taste of a chicken stock cube although it is of vegetable origin and is therefore useful in all types of soup.

GELATIN

Powdered gelatin is available in packets and is unflavoured. It is suitable for both sweet and savoury dishes (for use see Melon with Fresh Orange Jelly, p. 32). Ordinary gelatin is an animal derivative, so kosher gelatin, although sometimes difficult to obtain, is essential.

PASTRY

Phyllo pastry, sometimes called 'fila', is a paper-thin pastry obtainable in packets of 1 lb (450 g). It contains no fat and should therefore be brushed with oil or melted butter and is often used in layers to make Middle Eastern specialities.

Puff pastry has an equal proportion of fat (margarine or butter) to flour. Kosher puff pastry is available, but the home-made version is excellent if you have the time to make it.

WINES AND SPIRITS

For rabbinical reasons the making of wines, sherries and liqueurs with a grape content must be supervised by Jews, so in effect these must have a kosher label. Whisky, rum, gin and vodka are all permitted.

CHEESES

Soft cheeses like cream, cottage and curd cheese feature in many Jewish dishes, but you will not find recipes with any blue-veined cheese. Most hard cheese contains animal rennet in very small quantities, and this means that where a hard cheese like cheddar is mentioned it must be rennet-free.

HERBS AND SEASONING

Throughout the book the seasoning is left very much to personal taste, as it is impossible to give a general rule about salt and pepper. However, by pepper I always mean freshly-ground black pepper.

The use of garlic is also a controversial subject, as many people claim to detest it. One clove, crushed, is often enough to add a light flavouring to a dish. However, if you prefer, you may always leave it out.

I always like to use fresh or frozen herbs rather than dried ones. They have a less pronounced flavour but add a subtle finish rather than a strong, overpowering taste.

Glossary

adafina A hot, filling dish, cooked overnight for Sabbath lunch. The Sephardi version usually consists of beef brisket and chick peas.

bagels (or *beigels*) Bread rings which are made from a firm dough, boiled for a few minutes and then baked, and often served for breakfast on Sunday mornings.

blintzes Thin pancakes, filled with soft cheese or a savoury mixture.

challa (or *hallah*) Plaited white bread, enriched with egg and sprinkled with poppy seeds, always served at the Friday night meal.

charoset A mixture of nuts, apples and wine served at the Seder service on Passover.

cholent The Ashkenazi version of adafina (see above), also made with beef, but usually with barley, beans or potatoes.

falafel (or *felafel*) A popular Israeli snack, made from ground chick peas, fried into balls and served with pita bread.

frankfurters Short, thick all-beef sausages which just need to be boiled and peeled.

gefilte fish Raw, minced fish formed into patties and either fried or poached and served cold.

hamantaschen Triangular pastries, made of either yeast or pastry dough, usually with a poppy seed filling called 'mohn'—a traditional Purim cake.

helzel The skin of the chicken neck—often filled with stuffing and roasted or boiled with the chicken.

jemma A rich filling for sweets, made from egg yolks and sugar, and a favourite among Spanish and Portuguese Jews.

kuchen Cake (from the German), usually made with yeast but often referring now to the quick 'coffee cakes' where all the ingredients are mixed together at the same time.

latkes Potato cakes fried in oil.

lockshen Noodles or vermicelli—the very fine pasta used in soup or in lockshen pudding.

matzah (*or matzo*, pl. *matzot*) Flat, crisp unleavened bread for Passover.

matzo meal Meal made from grinding matzah which is often used instead of breadcrumbs. It may be fine-ground for cakes or medium-ground and slightly crunchy for coating.

schnitzel Thin escalopes or slices of meat, usually veal but nowadays often taken from the breast of a turkey.

smatana (*or smetana*) Sour cream of a thinner consistency, made from skimmed milk with added cream.

strudel The Hungarian or Austrian version implies paper-thin pastry, usually with an apple or cherry filling. Strudel biscuits are often made from a crumbly pastry with a dried fruit filling and are traditionally served after synagogue at Kiddush (Sanctification).

viennas All-beef sausages with no cereal added. They are generally boiled for five minutes to heat them through.

wursht Salami, served either raw and thinly sliced, or fried, when it is cut in thick chunks and often served with eggs.

Weights, Measures and Quantities

Metrication

All the recipes give the imperial (traditional) weights and measures first and the metric ones in brackets afterwards. This is because they were originally developed using the old system and have been converted, as nearly as possible, to the new metric system. However, as I have followed the general practice of using a table of grams to the nearest 25 g (and the precise conversion is 1 oz = 28·4 g) the equivalents are not always exact, and greater care should be taken when using the metric version in certain cakes, etc. where the amounts need to be more specific. Always bear in mind that metric quantities will be slightly smaller, and remember to follow either one set of measurements or the other and never try to mix the two.

For exact conversions, here is a table to follow:

oz/fl. oz	g and ml (to nearest number)	g (to nearest 25)
1	28	25
2	57	50
3	85	75
4	113	125
5 ($\frac{1}{4}$ pt)	142	150
6	170	175
7	198	200
8 ($\frac{1}{2}$ lb)	226	225
10 ($\frac{1}{2}$ pt)	283	275
12	340	350
15 ($\frac{3}{4}$ pt)	428	425
16 (1 lb)	456	450
20 (1 pt)	569	575

As a guide, 1 kilogram (1000 g) equals about 2 lb 3 oz and 1 litre (1000 ml) equals about $1\frac{3}{4}$ pints.

With liquid measures, small amounts are given in teaspoons and tablespoons.

Oven temperatures

These are given with the gas Regulo number first, followed by degrees in Fahrenheit and Celsius.

Measurements

These are given first in inches with centimetres in brackets. 1 inch equals 2·5 cm.

Quantities

Unless otherwise stated, the recipes are intended to serve approximately four people. Amounts, of course, vary with individual tastes and appetites. With cakes and desserts it is even more difficult to judge, and recipes given for these are more likely to serve six people as it is often not economical to make them in small sizes.

1. Hors d'Oeuvre

Appetizers are a fairly new idea in Jewish cooking, the most famous being chopped liver or herring. At celebration dinners the first course is often a fruit, like melon, pineapple or avocado. However, for meals at home a vegetable or salad makes a good start to a hot meal, while a soufflé or pastry is better with a cold main course. Many of the recipes in other sections make good starters and you may like to take some of the suggestions for Light Savoury Dishes and Snacks, perhaps varying the quantities slightly. The amounts given are always for four people, unless otherwise stated.

Fried Chicken Pick-ups (m)
Chopped Liver (m)
Avocados with Chicken Salad (m)
Stuffed Courgettes in Lemon Sauce (m) or (p)
Chicken Soufflé (m)
Salami Platter (m)
Pink Grapefruit Cocktail (p)
Melon with Fresh Orange Jelly (p)
Artichoke Squares (p)
Eggs Stuffed with Mushrooms (d) or (p)
Tomatoes in Cream Dressing (d)
Herring and Sour Cream Salad (d)

❋ Fried Chicken Pick-ups ❋ (m)

8 oz (225 g) raw chicken
1–2 eggs, beaten

    salt, pepper
    3 oz (75 g) matzo meal, medium-ground
    1 oz (25 g) sesame seeds (optional)
    oil for frying

Cut the chicken into finger-length pieces, dip each one into beaten egg and then coat with the seasoned matzo meal. (Sesame seeds may be mixed with the matzo meal to give a more crunchy finish.)

    Heat the oil in a deep pan and fry the chicken pieces for about 10 minutes, or until they are golden-brown. Either serve them immediately or reheat them on a baking sheet in a hot oven (gas mark 6, 400° F, 200° C) for about 10 minutes.

    This amount makes about 30.

❈ Chopped Liver ❈   (m)

This is a lighter version of the well-known dish, using very little fat.

    1 medium-sized onion, chopped
    ¾ oz (20 g) margarine or chicken fat
    8 oz (225 g) chicken livers, previously grilled
    ¼ pt (125 ml) chicken stock
    1 hardboiled egg
    salt, pepper

In a non-stick pan, sauté the chopped onion in the margarine or chicken fat for about 10 minutes. Over a medium heat stir it occasionally until it is a light golden colour. Then add the chicken livers and a little more fat if necessary. Turn up the heat, add the chicken stock and cook briskly until most of the liquid is absorbed. Remove the pan from the heat and then put the onion and liver mixture with the hardboiled egg through a mincer. There should be enough liquid to make a smooth pâté. Season to taste and leave to cool.

❊ Avocados with Chicken Salad ❊ (m)

This is an all-season starter, filling enough for winter, while the cool green colour makes it very attractive on a summer table.

2 ripe avocados
juice of ½ lemon
6 oz (175 g) chicken, cooked
6 oz (175 g) boiled potatoes, cubed
½ green pepper, chopped
2 fl oz (50 ml) mayonnaise
salt, pepper

For the garnish
shredded lettuce and cucumber slices

Halve the avocados, remove the stones and brush the flesh with the lemon juice. Cut the chicken into chunks, add the potatoes and chopped green pepper and mix together with the mayonnaise. Season to taste.

Pile the mixture into the avocado halves and place each one on a bed of shredded lettuce, garnished with cucumber slices.

❊ Stuffed Courgettes in Lemon Sauce ❊ (m) or (p)

1 lb (450 g) courgettes, halved
6 tbsps oil for frying
1 small onion, chopped
1 oz (25 g) rice
2 oz (50 g) pine nuts
pinch oregano
1 clove garlic, minced
salt, pepper
½ pt (¼ l) chicken stock*

For the lemon sauce
2 egg yolks

juice of $\frac{1}{2}$ lemon
3 fl oz (75 ml) chicken stock*
salt

Preheat the oven to gas mark 4, 350° F, 180° C. Scoop the centres out of the halved courgettes and sauté the halves in oil for a few minutes. Remove them to a greased overproof dish. For the filling, sauté the onion and chopped courgettes until they are golden, add the rice, pine nuts, oregano and seasoning and then cover with hot chicken stock.* Simmer for about 10 minutes until the rice is tender and then fill the courgettes with the mixture. Bake, covered, for about 40 minutes.

After about 30 minutes, prepare the sauce. Beat the egg yolks with the lemon juice in a bowl. Pour on the hot stock, season, and in a pan, over low heat, stir gently until the sauce thickens slightly. Do not boil, and as soon as it is thick, remove it from the heat and serve with the stuffed courgettes.

❋ Chicken Soufflé ❋ (m)

3 egg yolks
8 oz (225 g) cooked breast of chicken, minced
salt, pepper, paprika or cayenne
5 egg whites
2 oz (50 g) almonds, blanched and flaked

For the chicken sauce
2 oz (50 g) chicken fat or margarine
2 oz (50 g) flour
8 fl oz (225 ml) chicken soup or stock
salt, pepper

First make the chicken sauce. Melt the fat and add the flour, stirring well. Gradually add the stock and continue stirring

* Or use parev chicken stock powder, if you are serving with a dairy meal.

until the sauce thickens. Add the seasoning and leave to cool slightly.

Prepare an 8-in (20-cm) soufflé dish with a greased paper collar rising about 2 in (5 cm) above the rim of the dish. Preheat the oven to gas mark 5, 375° F, 190° C.

Add the egg yolks to the chicken sauce and then fold in the minced cooked chicken. Season with salt, pepper and a little paprika or cayenne. Make sure that the whites are at room temperature and whisk them until they are stiff but not dry. Then fold them into the chicken mixture, being careful not to stir too much as this will prevent the soufflé from rising. As soon as the egg whites are incorporated, spoon the mixture into the prepared dish and scatter over the almonds. Cook in the centre of the oven for 35 minutes without opening the door, and serve immediately.

❄ Salami Platter ❄ (m)

This is very like the Italian hors d'oeuvre, but omits the tuna fish and anchovies as it is a custom not to serve fish and meat together, in one course, at a Jewish table.

5 oz (150 g) smoked dry salami
4 oz (125 g) tinned artichoke hearts, drained
2 large tomatoes, quartered
4 oz (125 g) whole french beans, cooked
black and green olives

Slice the salami and arrange it on a platter with the artichoke hearts, tomatoes, french beans and small piles of black and green olives.

Serve with plenty of challa or fresh wholemeal bread.

❄ Pink Grapefruit Cocktail ❄ (p)

2 large pink grapefruit
2 small oranges

4 oz (125 g) large white grapes
sugar to taste
1 chinese gooseberry

Make small diagonal cuts around the centre of the grapefruit
and continue cutting until the two halves can be separated.
Remove the flesh of the fruit with a grapefruit knife and then
cut between the membranes to remove the segments. Place
these, together with the juice, into a bowl. Peel the oranges and
remove the segments from these too, being careful to avoid
the pith and membranes. Add the orange pieces to the grapefruit with the pipped white grapes, and add sugar to taste.
(Most pink grapefruits are sweet and sometimes no sugar is
needed at all.)

Spoon the fruit mixture with the juices back into the grapefruit shells and top each one with a slice of green chinese gooseberry. Chill well.

❋ Melon with Fresh Orange Jelly ❋ (p)

This is a refreshing starter which can equally well be served as
a dessert. It needs no sugar if the melon is ripe and sweet.

1 medium-sized honeydew melon or 2 small ogen melons
juice of 3–4 oranges
3–4 tbsps powdered kosher gelatin

To prepare kosher gelatin
Mix the powder with a few spoonfuls of juice in a small cup.
Then place the cup in a pan of hot water and stir over gentle
heat for a few minutes until the gelatin mixture softens. Then
use it, either hot to pour into a hot mixture, or cold in a cold one,
stirring well all the time to avoid stringiness.

Cut the flesh of the melon into dice or balls and place in a
bowl. Pour the juice into a measuring jug together with the
strained juice of the oranges (reserving a few spoonfuls to prepare the gelatin). When you have prepared the gelatin mixture,

cool it and pour it into the juice, making it up to $\frac{3}{4}$ pt (425 ml) with water.

Put the melon dice or balls into tall glasses and pour over the orange jelly. Refrigerate for a few hours until set.

❋ Artichoke Squares ❋ (p)

2 14-oz (400-g) tins artichokes
8 eggs
4 fl oz (125 ml) vegetable or chicken stock
salt, pepper

For the garnish
mayonnaise, radishes, gherkins

Chop the artichokes roughly and mix with the beaten eggs, stock and seasoning. Grease an 8 in × 10 in (20 cm × 25 cm) tin or ovenproof dish and bake at gas mark 5, 375° F, 190° C for about 45 minutes. Leave to cool, and then cut into squares.

The squares can either be served on their own, or covered with a thin layer of mayonnaise and decorated with slices of radish and gherkin.

❋ Eggs Stuffed with Mushrooms ❋ (d) or (p)

4 large eggs
1 tbsp onion, chopped
olive oil for frying
$\frac{1}{4}$ lb (125 g) small button mushrooms, sliced
salt, pepper, dash of sugar
$\frac{1}{2}$ tsp tomato purée
1 tbsp single cream or 2 tsps parev 'milk' powder mixed with
  2 tsps water

Hardboil the eggs, slice them in half lengthwise and mash the yolks. Sauté the chopped onion in a little oil, add the mushrooms, reserving a few slices for decoration. Season with the salt, pepper and sugar and add the tomato purée. Chop the mushroom mixture and mix it with the egg yolks. Stir in the cream (or the blended parev 'milk' powder) and pile the mixture into the cooked egg whites. Garnish with sliced mushrooms.

❖ Tomatoes in Cream Dressing ❖ (d)

This is an unusual and very delicate way of serving tomatoes, either as a first course or as a side salad with fish.

> *2 tsps oil*
> *juice of ½ lemon*
> *salt, pepper*
> *½ clove garlic*
> *4 large tomatoes, peeled*
> *1 tbsp chives and parsley, chopped*
> *2 tbsps whipped cream*

Mix the oil, lemon juice, salt and pepper in a screw-top jar and shake well. Add a cut piece of garlic clove and leave to allow the taste to infuse while you prepare the tomatoes.

Slice the tomatoes thinly and arrange them in a bowl. Pour a few spoonfuls of the dressing over the tomatoes and then cover with the whipped cream. Sprinkle with the chopped herbs and refrigerate for a while before serving.

❖ Herring and Sour Cream Salad ❖ (d)

I include this as a quick dish, but the authentic version would use herrings which have been pickled at home for several days.

> *4 pickled herrings*
> *1 small onion*
> *1 crisp eating apple, brushed with lemon juice*
> *¼ pt (150 ml) sour cream*

Drain the herrings well and cut them into wide strips. Arrange them on a serving dish. Slice the onion and blanch it for one minute in boiling water (or leave it raw and crisp if you like a stronger flavour). Slice the apple. Mix the herring with the apple and onion and cover with the sour cream.

Serve chilled with challa or fresh wholemeal bread.

2. Soups

For centuries soup has played an important part in Jewish cuisine. It is filling, warming, nearly always cheap and easy to make. In most of the recipes I use home-made stock. This gives a less pronounced but more delicate flavour than stock cubes which, although a convenient substitute, do not really create flavour, but merely add to it. It is a good idea to make the stock in advance as it keeps well in the refrigerator or freezer. When working out quantities you need to allow about $\frac{1}{3}$ pt (200 ml) per person.

All the meat-based soups and stocks may be simmered for hours, but those containing puréed vegetables will tend to stick to the base of the saucepan if left unattended. Do remember that stocks made with vegetables turn sour quickly so either freeze them immediately or refrigerate for only one day. All soups with milk or cream should be stirred carefully and heated only gently before serving.

Chicken Soup (m)
Tomato Rice Soup (m)
Carrot and Barley Soup (m)
Butter Bean Soup (m)
Giblet Soup (m)
Chilled Onion Soup (m)
Potato Soup (d)
Fresh Pea Soup with Mint (d)
Tomato Velvet Cream (d)
Chilled Beetroot Borscht (d)

✤ Chicken Soup ✤ (m)

This must be the most famous of all Jewish dishes. It should be made from a fresh boiling fowl which gives a much richer flavour than oven-ready roasters. Try to make it well in advance in order to remove all traces of fat.

1 5-lb (2-kg) boiling fowl (including the giblets and feet
 which should be blanched in boiling water and then skinned)
2 small onions
2 large carrots
5 stalks celery
3 pts (1½ l) cold water
salt, pepper

Place the chicken and the vegetables in a large deep soup pot. Add the water and bring it to the boil. Remove the froth which comes to the surface and skim carefully for a few minutes. Then add the seasonings, cover, and simmer over low heat for about 2 hours. If the chicken is tender remove it (otherwise leave for up to another hour) and when it is cool, take the meat off the bones and return the carcase to the soup. Continue cooking for a further hour. Strain the soup into a bowl and either refrigerate overnight or place in the freezer for a few hours. Remove the pale layer of fat which completely covers the top. The soup should set to a thick jelly when cold.

This can be used as stock in sauces or as chicken soup with any of the usual accompaniments. The boiled chicken can also be used in a variety of ways (see for example Chicken Pancakes, p. 61, or Chicken with Mushroom Sauce, p. 82).

Good accompaniments are knaidlach (see p. 147), kreplach (see p. 58), lockshen or noodles.

❊ Tomato Rice Soup ❊ (m)

This is one of those recipes which can be as easy and quick as you want to make it.

> ¾ pt (425 ml) tomato pulp (fresh or tinned tomatoes, sieved)
> ½ tsp celery salt
> 2 tbsps tomato purée
> 2 pts (1 l) beef stock or 3 beef stock cubes dissolved in
>   2 pts (1 l) water
> ½ tsp sugar
> salt, pepper
> 1 oz (25 g) rice

Put all the ingredients, except the rice, into a saucepan and bring to the boil. Simmer for about 30 minutes then add the rice. Continue boiling gently for about 10 minutes when the rice will be cooked and the soup will be a dark, rich colour. Taste for seasoning and serve hot.

❊ Carrot and Barley Soup ❊ (m)

> 1½ pts (¾ l) white veal stock, using veal bones
> 2 tbsps barley
> 3 medium-sized carrots
> 4 stalks celery
> 1 onion
> 1 oz (25 g) margarine or fat
> salt, pepper

First prepare a rich veal stock by simmering some veal bones for several hours in water. Strain the stock into a clean saucepan, add the barley and continue cooking until the barley is soft (about 2 hours or about 20 minutes in a pressure cooker).

Slice the carrot, celery and onion and sauté in the fat, stirring until golden. Pour on the barley and stock and if necessary add some water to make it up to about 2 pts (1 l). Season well.

✳ Butter Bean Soup ✳ (m)

8 oz (225 g) carrots, chopped
10 oz (275 g) onions, chopped
2 sticks celery, chopped
1 tbsp margarine or fat
1 lb (450 g) butter beans, previously soaked
1 pt ($\frac{1}{2}$ l) meat stock (beef or lamb)
salt, pepper

Sauté the chopped vegetables in the fat, turning them well to coat, and then cook them for about 10 minutes until they start to soften. Add the drained, soaked beans and pour on the meat stock. Then either pressure-cook for about 20 minutes or simmer for several hours until the beans are tender. Put the soup through a sieve or blend until smooth. Add a little more soup stock or water to make up to about 2 pts (1 l) and season to taste.

Serve very hot with croûtons or crisp bread or rolls.

✳ Giblet Soup ✳ (m)

If you have a freezer it is worth saving the giblets from 5 or 6 chickens to make this velvety soup.

chicken giblets (feet, necks, gizzards, etc.) from about 5
chickens or 2 turkeys
2 carrots
2 onions
salt, pepper
3–4 tbsps flour

Pour boiling water over the giblets, remove any skin and fat and drain them. Then place them in a saucepan or pressure cooker with the carrots, onions and seasoning and cover with cold water. Bring to the boil and skim off the white froth which will rise to the top. Then simmer the stock until the giblets are cooked (about 2 hours or 20 minutes in a pressure cooker). Pour the stock into a bowl and chill it.

Remove the fat from the surface of the stock and melt about 2 tbsps of it in a saucepan. Stir in about 3 tbsps flour, or enough to make a roux, and then pour the giblet stock on slowly, stirring all the time to make a thick, pale soup. Chop the giblets (discarding the feet and the bones) and add them to the soup. Be careful to stir while heating as a thickened soup tends to stick to the saucepan if left.

❊ Chilled Onion Soup ❊ (m)

This is an easy summer soup to prepare well in advance using mainly store cupboard ingredients.

> *2 large onions*
> *outer leaves from a large lettuce*
> *12 fl oz (350 ml) chicken stock or 1 chicken stock cube dissolved in 12 fl oz (350 ml) water*
> *3 medium-sized potatoes, cooked*
> *4 tbsps parev 'milk' powder*
> *½ tsp sugar*
> *salt, pepper*

> For the garnish
> *3–4 spring onions, chopped finely*

Peel and slice the onions and put them in a saucepan with the lettuce leaves and half the chicken stock. Cook until the onions are soft. Then place the potatoes with the rest of the chicken stock, the onion mixture and the parev 'milk' powder in a blender or sieve. Stir until the mixture is smooth and creamy and season well. If it is too thick, add a little more stock or water.

Chill the soup and just before serving garnish with spring onions.

✳ Potato Soup ✳ (d)

This soup is pale and creamy with strips of vegetables to add colour and taste.

> 3 large carrots
> 2 leeks
> 1 onion
> 2 stalks celery
> 1 oz (25 g) butter
> 3 medium-sized potatoes
> ½ pt (¼ l) creamy milk
> salt, pepper

First make a vegetable stock with 1½ carrots, 1½ leeks, ½ onion and the celery. Place them all in a pan and cover with water. Bring to the boil and simmer for about an hour.

Meanwhile shred the remaining onion, leek and carrot into julienne strips and sauté them in butter. Cook the potatoes in a little salted water and drain them.

Then put the potatoes, milk and stock (which should measure about ¾ pt/425 ml) into a blender or through a sieve until the mixture is a smooth white purée. Add the vegetable strips, reheat gently, adjust seasoning and serve hot.

✳ Fresh Pea Soup with Mint ✳ (d)

> ½ onion, chopped
> 1 stick celery, chopped
> 1½ oz (40 g) butter
> 1 lb (450 g) fresh peas (after shelling)
> 1 bunch fresh mint
> 1 pt (½ l) water or vegetable stock
> ½ pt (¼ l) milk

For the garnish
4 tbsps single cream
mint, parsley or chives, chopped

Sauté the onion and celery in the butter until they are a light golden colour. Add the shelled peas and several leaves of mint. Then pour on the stock or water, season well and simmer until the vegetables are tender. Remove the mint leaves and sieve or blend the mixture to make a thick purée. Heat the milk and add this to the purée, stirring well. Taste for seasoning.

Serve very hot in individual bowls garnished with a swirl of cream and chopped mint, parsley or chives.

❊ Tomato Velvet Cream ❊ (d)

This soup is based on a bechamel sauce, which is very useful in Jewish cookery. As dairy products are never combined with meat, many other dishes like fish, pasta and pastries make full use of butter and milk.

2 oz (50 g) butter
1 oz (25 g) flour
¾–1 pt (425–550 ml) milk
1 onion, chopped
1 carrot, chopped
1 lb (450 g) fresh tomatoes, skinned and chopped
salt, pepper
1 tsp sugar
3 tsps tomato purée
½ pt (¼ l) vegetable stock

For serving
¼ pt (150 ml) single cream
4 tbsps sherry

First make the bechamel sauce. Melt 1 oz (25 g) butter in a small saucepan, stir in 1 oz (25 g) flour and mix well. Then gradually pour on $\frac{1}{2}$ pt ($\frac{1}{4}$ l) milk (warm milk mixes better) and continue stirring until the sauce thickens. Add seasoning and remove from heat.

Sauté the onion and carrot in 1 oz (25 g) butter. When they are slightly coloured and beginning to soften, add the tomatoes. Season with salt, pepper and sugar and add the tomato purée and vegetable stock. Simmer for about 30 minutes until the vegetables are tender.

Pass the mixture through a sieve or blender and then stir in the bechamel sauce. Adjust the seasoning and add enough extra milk to make a smooth soup.

Reheat before serving, stirring all the time, and to each bowl of soup add a swirl of sherry and single cream.

❈ Chilled Beetroot Borscht ❈   (d)

Borscht is of Russian or Polish origin and is made from cabbage or beetroot. Often it has a beef stock base, but this one is very simple and quick. It looks pretty and is very cooling on a summer day.

> *6 large beetroots, uncooked*
> *1 small onion*
> *2 pts (1 l) water*
> *2 tbsps sugar*
> *2 tsps salt*
> *pepper*
> *2 eggs*
> *juice of 1 lemon*

> For serving
> *5 fl oz (125 ml) sour cream*

Peel and grate the beetroots and the onion and cover with the water and seasoning. Bring to the boil and simmer for about 40 minutes. Strain the soup and pour it gradually on to the beaten eggs, stirring all the time. Then add the lemon juice, return to the heat and stir until the soup is hot, but be careful not to let it boil. After it has thickened leave it to get quite cold.

Serve it in bowls or glasses with a thick swirl of sour cream.

3. Fish

❋❋❋

To our grandparents 'fish' meant gefilte fish—which was literally 'stuffed fish', a tasty way of extending the freshwater fish that was available to them. In England, where there is an abundance of fresh fish, Jews have developed a greater interest in cooking it, and wherever there is a Jewish community you will be sure to find an excellent fish shop. The most important thing is that the fish should be absolutely fresh. The traditional recipes will always be good for festivals, but most of the newer ones I have chosen take very little time and are suitable for simple family meals or dinner parties.

Fried Fish (p)
Gefilte Fish Balls (p)
Soused Herrings or Mackerel (p)
Smoked and Pickled Fish: Marinated Kippers, Pickled Salmon (p)
Baked Trout (p)
Fresh Salmon Mousse (d)
Trout with Cucumber Balls (d)
Halibut Steaks with Mushrooms (d)
Halibut or Hake with Wine and Cheese Sauce (d)
Fish and Asparagus Flan (d)
Lemon Sole with Spinach (d)
Creamed Fish: Fish Pie, Fish Croquettes (d)
Rolled Fish Fillets in Whole Tomatoes (d)

❖ Fried Fish ❖ (p)

In Jewish homes, fried fish is nearly always served cold because it is one of the most successful ways of cooking fish for Sabbaths and festivals. If you have never tried it, you are missing one of the real Jewish specialities. The amounts given are enough for about 8 people as it is hardly worth doing less. Whichever fish you choose must be absolutely fresh.

> 8 large fillets of cod, haddock or lemon sole or 8 small whole
>   dover sole or halibut steaks or 3 very large whole plaice, cut
>   into three across
> a pan of oil about 2 in (5 cm) deep at a temperature of 375° F
>   (190° C)
> 4 eggs, beaten
> about 6 tbsps matzo meal, medium-ground
> salt, pepper

Wash and dry the fish very well. Heat the oil and have ready two plates—one with beaten egg and the other with seasoned matzo meal. Cover the fish with the matzo meal and then dip it immediately into the beaten egg and lower it carefully into the hot oil. Cook it for about 6 to 8 minutes according to thickness and when it is golden-brown, take it out and drain it very well. Place the cooked fish on kitchen paper to absorb any surplus oil and continue cooking the rest of the fish. Leave to cool and serve cold. It will keep for up to two days (or can be frozen) but will be at its best and crispest on the day it is cooked.

❖ Gefilte Fish Balls ❖ (p)

There are two types of gefilte fish—fried and boiled. There are also many different versions, but this mixture makes delicious, crisply coated small balls to serve as an appetizer.

> 1 lb (450 g) fish (pike, carp, bream, haddock, cod, whiting or
>   a mixture of any of these), minced

1 onion, grated or minced
1 egg, beaten
salt, pepper
1–2 tsps sugar (according to taste)
5–6 tbsps matzo meal, medium-ground
oil for frying

Mix the minced fish with the onion, beaten egg and seasoning. Add a little matzo meal and form the mixture into small balls. Roll the balls in the rest of the meal and leave in a cool place until you are ready to fry them. Heat some oil in a deep pan (see Fried Fish, p. 46) and fry the balls for about 8 minutes or until they are golden-brown. Drain them well and leave them to get cold.

❊ Soused Herrings or Mackerel ❊ (p)

6 herrings or mackerel, split open
1 Spanish onion
salt, pepper
1 dsp sugar
4 peppercorns
2 bay leaves, crushed
1 dsp black treacle
¾ pt (425 ml) white vinegar and water (½ of each)

Wash the herrings and scrape them well, removing as many bones as possible. Chop the onion into small pieces and put a small spoonful on each herring fillet. Season with salt and pepper, roll up and secure with a cocktail stick. Place in a baking dish with the rest of the onion and add the sugar, peppercorns, bay leaves and treacle. Pour over the vinegar and water mixture and bake at gas mark 4, 350° F, 180° C for 10 minutes. Turn the oven down to gas mark 2, 300° F, 150° C and continue cooking until the fish is golden-brown—about three-quarters of an hour. Serve cold.

❊ Smoked and Pickled Fish ❊ (p)

Because fresh fish has to be eaten on the day it is cooked, Jewish recipes often use smoked or pickled fish, varying from relatively cheap herrings to the very expensive smoked salmon. Here are two recipes you can try at home—though strictly speaking they are not traditional ones.

MARINATED KIPPERS

4 thick kipper fillets
4 tbsps olive oil
2 tbsps wine vinegar
2 tbsps parsley, chopped
black pepper

Mix together the oil and vinegar. Slice the kipper fillets very thinly and leave to soak overnight in the refrigerator, in the oil and vinegar mixture. Next day, drain well, sprinkle with the parsley and pepper and serve with brown bread and butter.

PICKLED SALMON

2 lb (900 g) fresh salmon or salmon trout, cleaned
1 oz (25 g) sugar
1 oz (25 g) coarse salt
15 crushed white peppercorns
1 tbsp fresh dill (or $\frac{1}{4}$ tsp dried)

For the sauce
3 tbsps wine vinegar
1 tbsp sugar
2 tbsps dill, chopped (or $\frac{1}{2}$ tsp dried)
$1\frac{1}{2}$ tbsps continental mustard
4 fl oz (120 ml) oil

Cut the fish in half lengthwise and remove the backbone carefully. Rub both sides with a mixture of the sugar, salt, pepper and dill and wrap it in transparent film. Place it in the refrigerator and leave it for at least 2 days, turning it about 6 times. Scrape off the dill mixture, slice the salmon thinly, and serve with wholemeal or brown bread and mustard sauce.

To make the sauce, mix the vinegar, sugar, dill and mustard and add the oil slowly until it is the consistency of mayonnaise.

❧ Baked Trout ❧ (p)

You will need a whole fish for each person. Sometimes you can find delicately coloured pink trout which, although small, have the taste of salmon or sea trout.

> $\frac{1}{4}$ *pt (150 ml) fish stock made from :*
> $\frac{1}{2}$ *onion, chopped*
> $\frac{1}{2}$ *carrot, chopped*
> $\frac{1}{2}$ *pt ($\frac{1}{4}$ l) water*
>   *fish bones*
> *or $\frac{1}{4}$ pt (150 ml) dry white wine*
> *4 trout, cleaned*
> *salt, pepper*

If you are using fish stock, simmer the bones with the water and onion and carrot in a covered saucepan for about 30 minutes. Strain the stock and then continue cooking it over high heat to reduce it to about $\frac{1}{4}$ pt (150 ml). Alternatively, use wine instead of the stock.

In a shallow, greased ovenproof dish, place the trout in a single layer. Pour over the fish stock or wine and season well. Bake in a preheated oven at gas mark 7, 425° F, 220° C, for about 10 minutes, then turn off the oven and leave the fish in for a further 30 minutes. By this time the flesh will be cooked but not dry and the stock will almost have disappeared.

Remove the fish carefully to a serving dish and lift the skin off (it will come away quite easily). The fish can either be served hot with buttered new potatoes and slices of lemon, or left to cool, when it is delicious with a salad and mayonnaise.

❖ Fresh Salmon Mousse ❖   (d)

This makes a delicious summer buffet dish or may be served
as a starter for a dinner party. Either way, it is best made with
freshly cooked or leftover salmon, rather than using tinned
salmon.

> *1 tbsp kosher gelatin*
> *juice of ½ lemon*
> *8–12 oz (225–350 g) salmon, cooked*
> *2 eggs, separated*
> *1 tbsp real mayonnaise*
> *6 fl oz (175 ml) double cream*
> *salt, pepper*

> For decoration
> *slices of radish, cucumber and extra mayonnaise*

Prepare the gelatin (see notes in Melon with Fresh Orange
Jelly, p. 32), using the lemon juice or, alternatively, a few
tablespoons of the liquid in which the fish was cooked. Leave
the gelatin to cool. Mix the flaked salmon, egg yolks, mayonnaise
and seasoning and add the cooled gelatin, stirring very carefully.
Whisk the cream and the egg whites separately until they are
stiff, and then fold them into the salmon mixture. Spoon the
mousse into a greased fish-shaped mould or into small individual pots and leave to chill.

When it is set (this takes about 2 to 3 hours) turn it out and
garnish with slices of cucumber and radish and serve with a
little extra mayonnaise.

❖ Trout with Cucumber Balls ❖   (d)

> *4 trout, cleaned*
> *2 tbsps flour*
> *salt, pepper*

4 oz (125 g) butter
1 cucumber, peeled and scooped into balls
1 tbsp oil
2 tbsps single cream or top of the milk
1 tbsp parsley, chopped

Dry the fish very well and then toss it in seasoned flour. Heat 2 oz (50 g) of the butter in a heavy frying-pan and sauté the cucumber balls, turning them frequently for about 5 minutes. Put them into a serving dish and keep them warm while you cook the fish. Heat the rest of the butter with the oil and then fry the trout, over high heat, on both sides, until they are crisp and brown. This will take about 6 minutes. Take care that the butter does not burn and add a little more oil, if necessary. Season the fish well and then pour over the cream.

Remove the trout to the serving dish, surround it with the cucumber balls and stir the chopped parsley into the cream and buttery juices. Pour the sauce over the fish and serve immediately.

❊ Halibut Steaks with Mushrooms ❊ (d)

4 large, thick halibut steaks
salt, pepper
1 oz (25 g) butter
6 oz (175 g) dark mushrooms, sliced
¼ pt (150 ml) double cream

Place the fish on a greased rack in a grill pan and season well. Soften the butter and spread it all over the fish steaks and then grill them for about 5 minutes. Slice the mushrooms, place them on the fish and continue grilling on the other side until the fish is cooked (about another 5 to 10 minutes). If necessary, add a little more butter or spoon over the juices to prevent the mushrooms from drying out.

Whip the cream and have ready a hot serving dish. Remove

the halibut steaks to the dish, surround with the sliced mush-rooms and top with the whipped cream. The heat of the fish and the buttery juices will melt the cream, so serve the halibut straight away with some new potatoes or fresh bread.

The following five recipes are all based on bechamel sauce (see Tomato Velvet Cream, p. 42) which goes particularly well with fish.

❊ Halibut or Hake with Wine and Cheese Sauce ❊ (d)

4 steaks or thick fillets hake, halibut, cod or haddock
salt, pepper
8½ fl oz (250 ml) dry white wine
5 tbsps thick bechamel sauce (see Tomato Velvet Cream, p. 42)
4 heaped tbsps grated cheese

Place the fish in a greased ovenproof dish, season carefully and cover with the wine. Cook in a preheated oven at gas mark 4, 350° F, 180° C, for about 10 minutes, then pour the wine into a small saucepan, leaving the fish in the oven dish. Bring the wine to the boil, reduce it to about half its original quantity and then stir in the bechamel sauce. Pour the wine mixture over the fish and sprinkle over the grated cheese. Return to the oven for a further 10 minutes and serve when the cheese sauce is bubbling.

❊ Fish and Asparagus Flan ❊   (d)

For the basic rich pastry
5 oz (125 g) margarine
8 oz (200 g) plain flour
1 egg yolk (reserve a little for glazing)
4 tbsps iced water

For the filling
8 oz (225 g) cooked white fish
*1 8-oz (225-g) tin asparagus tips or fresh or frozen asparagus,
   chopped*
¼ pt (150 ml) bechamel sauce (see Tomato Velvet Cream, p. 42)

First make the pastry. Rub the margarine into the flour and
mix to a dough with the egg yolk and water. Chill in the
refrigerator.

Roll out the pastry and line an 8-in (20-cm) flan case with it.
Roll out the trimmings and cut these into small fish shapes.
Bake the flan case blind and also cook the fish shapes until they
are golden at gas mark 7, 425° F, 220° C.

Meanwhile mix the fish with half the asparagus, and bind
with the bechamel sauce. When the flan case is cooked, spoon
in the fish and asparagus mixture. Decorate the top with the
rest of the asparagus and the pastry fishes and heat through in
the oven at gas mark 4, 350° F, 180° C, taking care that the
filling does not dry out, and keeping it covered if necessary.

❀ Lemon Sole with Spinach ❀ (d)

6 fillets lemon sole
½ pt (¼ l) white wine or fish stock
1 lb (450 g) fresh spinach
salt, pepper
2 oz (50 g) butter
2 oz (50 g) flour
½ pt (¼ l) milk or single cream
3 oz (75 g) cheese, grated

Place the rolled up fish fillets in a shallow pan and cover with
white wine or fish stock (see Baked Trout, p. 49). Simmer
gently for about 10 minutes or until the fish is opaque. Cook
the washed spinach for about 10 minutes over low heat, without
adding any extra water. Drain and season well and chop it
roughly. Butter a fairly shallow ovenproof dish and place the

cooked spinach on the base, then carefully lay the drained fillets on top.

Make a bechamel sauce (see Tomato Velvet Cream, p. 42) with the butter, flour and milk or cream and add some of the strained juice from the fish, stirring all the time. Pour the sauce over the fish and add the grated cheese. Place it under a hot grill for a few minutes to brown the top or heat the dish in a hot oven (gas mark 7, 425° F, 220° C) if it has been allowed to cool.

Serve with creamed or buttered new potatoes.

❈ Creamed Fish ❈ (d)

The mixture is the same for making fish pie or croquettes. Either way it is an ideal way of making up fish which can then be frozen really successfully.

FISH PIE

> *4 large fillets fresh haddock or cod*
> *¼ pt (150 ml) milk*
> *salt, pepper*
> *1 pt (½ l) bechamel sauce (see Tomato Velvet Cream, p. 42)*
> *2 tbsps fresh parsley, chopped*
> *1 lb (450 g) potatoes*
> *1 oz (25 g) butter*

FISH CROQUETTES

> *4 large fillets haddock or cod*
> *¼ pt (150 ml) milk*
> *salt, pepper*
> *½ pt (¼ l) bechamel sauce (see Tomato Velvet Cream, p. 42)*
> *2 tbsps fresh parsley, chopped*
> *½ lb (225 g) potatoes*
> *2 eggs, beaten*
> *4 tbsps matzo meal, medium-ground*
> *oil for frying*

Poach the fillets of fish in a pan with the milk and seasoning. After about 5 minutes it should be opaque. (Don't overcook it.) Drain it well and then flake it with a fork and mix in the bechamel sauce and chopped parsley. Cook the potatoes and mash them well.

For the pie, add the butter to the potatoes and put the fish mixture into a pie dish, covering it with piped creamed potato. Heat through in the oven or brown under the grill to crisp the potato topping.

For the croquettes, cook the fish as above and then mix it with the sauce and the mashed potatoes. The mixture should be of a firm consistency. When it is quite cold, form it into balls or croquettes and then roll each one first in beaten egg and then in matzo meal. Shallow-fry in hot oil, turning each one until they are golden-brown (about 5 minutes). Drain well and serve hot or cold.

❊ Rolled Fish Fillets in Whole Tomatoes ❊ (d)

4 whole plaice, sole or lemon sole, skinned and halved (making 8 fillets)
½ pt (¼ l) fish stock (see Baked Trout, p. 49)
16 tomatoes
2 oz (50 g) cheese, grated
2 oz (50 g) breadcrumbs, toasted
salt, pepper

For the 2 sauces
2 oz (50 g) flour
2 oz (50 g) butter
6 tbsps single cream
2 tsps tomato purée
2 tsps fresh herbs, chopped
6 tbsps sherry

Cut the fillets in half lengthwise and roll them up. Arrange them, touching, in a shallow pan and cover with fish stock. Poach them for about 10 minutes, turning them over once carefully until they are opaque.

Meanwhile plunge the tomatoes into boiling water, skin them and remove the tops and centres. Reserve the tops and chop the tomato pulp roughly.

Drain the cooked fillets and reserve the fish stock. Sprinkle a mixture of grated cheese and breadcrumbs in the base of each tomato and then put in the rolled fish. Put on the tomato tops and place the stuffed tomatoes in a greased ovenproof dish. Cook at gas mark 4, 350° F, 180° C for about 15 minutes while you prepare the sauces.

Make a bechamel sauce (see Tomato Velvet Cream, p. 42) with the flour, butter and single cream and some of the fish stock. For the tomato sauce, boil together the tomato pulp, tomato purée, seasoning and herbs for about 10 minutes. Pass through a sieve and stir in the sherry.

When the tomatoes are cooked, serve half of them with the bechamel sauce over the top and the rest with the tomato sauce.

4. Light Savoury Dishes and Snacks

Kosher restaurants are not generally renowned for their steaks or sauces. They specialize in the type of food which often serves as a snack at home, like salt beef sandwiches and viennas (see Glossary) and chips. Salt beef is really best served hot from a very large joint but in these days of smaller families one isn't likely to have a huge piece of beef simmering in the pot.

I have chosen some dishes which are good with cold meat or fish and some which are equally good on their own and need only a tossed salad on the side and fresh fruit to follow.

Quantities depend on whether you are making 'just a snack' and, of course, on what else you are serving at the meal. In my usual estimate of what is enough for four people, I have not allowed for second helpings!

Kreplach (m)
Sausage Puff Rings (m)
Minced Meat 'Cigarettes' (m)
Turkey and Grape Salad (m)
Chicken Pancakes (m)
Fried Rice Balls (m)
Cannelloni (m)
Potato Latkes (p)
Falafel (p)
Crispy Fried Pancakes (p)
Vegetable Risotto (d) or (p)
Asparagus Soufflé (d)
Cheese Blintzes (d)
Pasta Shells with Tomato Cream Sauce (d)

Cheese and Almond Squares (d)
Borekas: Cheese Borekas, Spinach Borekas (d)
Corn Horns (d)

❊ Kreplach ❊ (m)

These are small squares of filled dough which are usually served in chicken soup. However, if you serve them with tomato sauce they are very like Italian ravioli.

For the dough
4 oz (125 g) plain flour
pinch salt
1 egg
cold water

For the filling
$\frac{1}{4}$ lb (125 g) cooked meat (beef or lamb), minced
2 tbsps meat stock

For the tomato sauce
1 Spanish onion
1 tbsp oil
1 14-oz (400-g) can tomatoes
2 tbsps tomato purée
salt, pepper, sugar

Mix the flour and salt together and make a well in the centre. Beat the egg with 2 eggcupfuls of cold water and pour this into the well and then mix in the flour until it forms a soft dough. Knead for a few minutes and then leave the dough, covered, to rest for about 20 minutes. Flour a board liberally and roll out the dough *very thinly*—it should almost be transparent. Divide it in half. Place small spoonfuls of the meat, moistened with a little stock, at 2-in (5-cm) intervals all over one half of the dough. Lift the other half carefully and lay it on top, pressing it down around each spoonful of meat. Then cut it across and downwards, making small squares, and place these on a board to dry for about an hour.

Meanwhile make the tomato sauce. Chop the onion finely and sauté it in the oil. When it is just turning golden, add the tomatoes and the tomato purée and season well with salt, pepper and sugar to taste. Bring to the boil and then simmer for about 30 minutes.

Bring a large pan of water to the boil, add salt and boil the kreplach for about 10 to 15 minutes. Drain them well and serve with the tomato sauce poured generously over the top.

Alternatively, boil the kreplach in chicken soup and serve 2 or 3 with each portion of soup.

❋ Sausage Puff Rings ❋ (m)

8 oz (225 g) puff pastry
8 beef sausages

Roll the pastry out thinly on a floured board and cut it into strips about 1½ in (4 cm) wide and the length of a sausage. Remove the skin from the sausages and cut them lengthwise into two or three pieces, depending on how large they are.

Then place a length of sausage along each piece of pastry and pinch the sides together. Twist the enclosed sausage round to form a circle and seal the ends together with your fingers. (No water should be necessary—just flour your hands if they get sticky.) Then make a few cuts round the outside of the circle and place the sausage rounds on an ungreased baking sheet. Use up all the rest of the pastry and the sausages and bake in a hot oven (gas mark 7, 425° F, 220° C), for about 20 minutes or until the rings are puffed and golden. Eat straight from the oven.

❋ Minced Meat 'Cigarettes' ❋ (m)

8 oz basic rich pastry (see Fish and Asparagus Flan, p. 52)

For the meat filling
8 oz (225 g) lean beef, minced

1 onion, finely chopped
½ pt (¼ l) beef stock or *1 beef stock cube dissolved in ½ pt (¼ l)*
water
1 tbsp tomato purée
1 tsp sugar
salt, pepper

Make the pastry and chill in the refrigerator while you are preparing the filling.

In a non-stick pan cook the minced beef over a fairly high heat and pour away some of the fat that will appear. When the meat is brown, transfer it to a saucepan and use the remaining fat in the pan to sauté the onion. Then add this, with the stock (or stock cube and water), tomato purée and seasoning to the minced beef. Cook over low heat for about an hour. Strain off any juices and remove the fat before mixing them in again with the meat.

When the filling has cooled, roll out thin strips of the pastry, about 1½ in (4 cm) wide, and place a thin line of the cold minced meat mixture along each strip of pastry. Seal the ends together with your fingers to form long thin sausages and then cut them into cigarette lengths. Place these, seam side down, on a baking sheet. Brush with beaten egg and bake in a preheated oven (gas mark 7, 425° F, 220° C) for about 20 minutes. Serve straight away or leave to cool and reheat again just before the meal.

This amount makes about 48, and will serve about 12 as a snack with drinks or about 6 as a savoury with salad.

❈ Turkey and Grape Salad ❈   (m)

8 oz (225 g) cooked roast turkey
1 tbsp boiling water
1 tbsp parev 'milk' powder
2 fl oz (50 ml) mayonnaise
8 oz (225 g) white grapes
1 small Webb or iceberg lettuce

For the garnish
parsley

Cut the roast turkey into fairly large chunks. Peel and remove the pips from the grapes. Mix the boiling water with the parev 'milk' powder to make a cream and when it has cooled add it to the mayonnaise—this is to remove the tartness and blends very well with the flavour of the grapes.

Fold the mayonnaise into the turkey, add the grapes and arrange in mounds on a platter surrounded with chunks of crispy lettuce. Decorate the dish with parsley and chill well until ready to serve.

❄ Chicken Pancakes ❄ (m)

For the pancakes
4 oz (125 g) plain flour
2 tsps salt
2 eggs
2 tsps oil
8 fl oz (225 ml) water
extra oil for frying

For the sauce and filling
2 oz (50 g) chicken fat or margarine
2 oz (50 g) flour
½ pt (¼ l) chicken stock
1 lb (450 g) boiled chicken, diced
8 oz (225 g) flat mushrooms
½ oz (15 g) margarine

First make the pancake mixture. Put the flour and salt into a bowl and make a well in the centre. Gradually add the eggs and some of the oil and water and beat till smooth. Add the rest of the liquid and stir to make a lump-free batter. (If you have a blender all the ingredients can be whizzed together in a few seconds.) Grease a small frying-pan and fry the pancakes in a little oil until all the batter has been used.

Make the chicken sauce (see Chicken Soufflé, p. 30) with the fat, flour and chicken stock. Divide it in half, mix the chicken with one half and use this to fill the pancakes. Roll them up and place them in a greased, ovenproof dish. Melt the $\frac{1}{2}$ oz (15 g) margarine and sauté the chopped mushrooms in the fat until the juices start to run. Then add the rest of the chicken sauce and a little more stock if necessary to make a smooth pouring mixture.

Serve the pancakes hot (heated through in a moderate oven if they have been allowed to get cold) with the mushroom sauce poured over the top.

❊ Fried Rice Balls ❊   (m)

This is a favourite dish among Jews from both Italy and Libya.

> *12 oz (350 g) rice*
> *2 chicken livers, grilled*
> *1 tbsp chicken fat*
> *2 eggs, beaten*
> *salt, pepper*
> *3 tbsps dry breadcrumbs or matzo meal, medium-ground*
> *oil for frying*
> *$\frac{1}{2}$ pt ($\frac{1}{4}$ l) tomato sauce (see Kreplach, p. 58)*

Boil the rice in plenty of salted water for about 7 minutes, then drain it well and rinse it in cold water. Sauté the chicken livers in the fat and chop them roughly. Mix the rice, livers and 1 beaten egg together and form into balls. Season well. Roll the balls in beaten egg and then in crumbs or matzo meal. Chill well for at least 1 hour.

Have ready a pan of oil and deep-fry the rice balls for about 5 to 10 minutes, or until they are golden. Drain them well and serve with sieved tomato sauce on the side.

❊ Cannelloni ❊   (m)

The real Italian version of this dish is with minced meat and a cheese sauce. It works well with the chicken sauce and a tomato-flavoured filling.

> For the cannelloni
> *8 oz (225 g) cannelloni tubes*
> *8 oz (225 g) cooked beef or lamb, minced*
> *2 tbsps tomato purée*
> *salt, pepper*
>
> For the sauce
> *3 tbsps margarine or chicken fat*
> *3 tbsps flour*
> *1 pt ($\frac{1}{2}$ l) chicken stock*

Boil the cannelloni for about 10 to 15 minutes in salted water until they are cooked but not soft. Drain them and rinse in cold water. Mix the cooked, minced meat with the tomato purée, taste for seasoning and stuff the pasta tubes with the meat filling. Place the cannelloni in a single layer in a greased ovenproof dish.

Make a thin chicken sauce with the fat, flour and chicken stock (see Chicken Soufflé, p. 30) and pour it over the cannelloni. Heat at gas mark 5, 375° F, 190° C until the sauce is bubbling.

❧ Potato Latkes ❧ (p)

A traditional Chanucah dish—my version is one with no flour, making it *slightly* less fattening! Latkes can be made just before the meal and kept warm in the oven, but they are really at their best served straight from the pan and are often eaten with viennas or wursht (see Glossary).

> *16 oz (450 g) potatoes (about 4 medium-sized)*
> *$\frac{1}{2}$ onion, grated*
> *salt, pepper*
> *1 egg*
> *oil for frying*

First prepare the potatoes. Peel and grate them finely into a bowl of cold water (to prevent them from discolouring). Then put them in a sieve and run cold water through until it is no longer cloudy and squeeze them dry.

Mix the potato with the grated onion, salt and pepper and add the beaten egg. Heat a frying pan with enough oil to cover the bottom and put in spoonfuls of the potato mixture, pressing it down well. After about 5 minutes, turn the latkes over and fry on the other side. Drain well and serve.

This amount makes about 12 small latkes.

❋ Falafel ❋ (p)

These are small fried balls of ground chick peas. In Israel they are served as a snack on every street corner. Pita bread is cut in half and filled with the falafel balls, salad and tehina (sesame seed) sauce. You can buy the sauce in cans, and if you are feeling lazy, there is quite a good packet mix for the falafel!

8 oz (225 g) chick peas
1 tbsp oil
1 egg
2 cloves garlic, minced
1 tsp cumin
⅛ tsp chilli powder
¼ tsp coriander
1 tsp salt
4–8 tbsps matzo meal, medium-ground
extra oil for frying

Soak the chick peas overnight and then mince them finely. Mix together the oil, egg, garlic, salt and spices and add to the chick pea mixture. Bind together with enough matzo meal to make a thick batter which you can form into 1-in (2½-cm) balls. Deep-fry in very hot oil until they are brown, drain well and serve hot.

❋ Crispy Fried Pancakes ❋ (p)

12 pancakes (see Chicken Pancakes, p. 61)

1 onion
1 carrot
2 sticks celery
1 tbsp oil
1 tbsp soy sauce
1 tsp tomato purée
8 oz (225 g) bean sprouts
1 egg
extra oil for frying

First make the pancakes and cook them on one side only. Place them cooked side up on greaseproof paper while you prepare the filling.

Chop the onion, carrot and celery finely and sauté them in the tablespoon of oil, stirring until they are golden-brown. Add the soy sauce and tomato purée and then add the bean sprouts. Stir-fry for about a minute and then set aside to cool.

Place a spoonful of the cooled filling on to the cooked side of each pancake. Fold over each side and then roll into a small parcel, sealing the edges with a little beaten egg. Heat a pan of oil and fry the pancakes carefully until they are crisp and golden. Drain well and serve hot.

❊ **Vegetable Risotto** ❊   **(d)** or **(p)**

4 oz (125 g) mushrooms
4 oz (125 g) french beans
2 carrots
1 fat spring onion
1 oz (25 g) butter or margarine
1 tbsp oil
6 oz (175 g) rice, soaked in cold water for ½ hour and drained
8 fl oz (225 ml) vegetable stock
8 fl oz (225 ml) dry cider or white wine
salt, pepper

For serving
knob of butter or margarine
grated cheese (optional)

Chop the mushrooms, beans, carrots and spring onion finely and sauté them in a heavy pan until they are coated with the butter and beginning to turn brown. Add a little oil if necessary, sprinkle in the rice and stir well. Pour on the vegetable stock and the dry cider or wine and add the seasoning. Cover with a tight-fitting lid and cook over very low heat until the liquid has been absorbed (about 10 to 15 minutes). If the rice is not quite cooked add some more liquid, but do not allow the rice to become mushy.

Finish with a knob of butter and a sprinkling of black pepper and grated cheese, and serve immediately.

Note : the risotto can be 'parev' by omitting the butter and cheese but it is not as good.

❋ Asparagus Soufflé ❋ (d)

This soufflé can be made with any vegetable—spinach, cauliflower, leeks and mushrooms all give a good flavour.

3 tbsps butter
4 tbsps flour
12 fl oz (350 ml) milk
6 egg yolks
4–5 tbsps cheese, grated
salt, pepper
1 tbsp fresh herbs (parsley or chives), chopped
6 oz (175 g) cooked asparagus, or other cooked vegetable
8 egg whites

Butter an 8-in (20-cm) soufflé dish and tie a paper collar round it, so that it rises a few inches above the rim. Heat the oven to gas mark 4, 350° F, 180° C.

Make a bechamel sauce (see Tomato Velvet Cream, p. 42).

with the butter, flour and milk and stir in the egg yolks, one at a time. Then add the grated cheese, seasoning, herbs and chopped cooked asparagus. Whisk the egg whites until stiff but not dry and fold them very carefully and gently into the asparagus mixture. Pile it into the soufflé dish and cook for 35 to 40 minutes. The soufflé is done when it is well risen and brown on top and does not wobble if you shake the dish slightly. Serve it *immediately* it is cooked.

❖ Cheese Blintzes ❖   (d)

A 'blintz' is a traditional pancake and the cheese filling can be sweet or savoury. Some people like to sprinkle more sugar on top too. The little parcels can be prepared in advance, frozen or refrigerated, and fried just before serving.

> *12 pancakes (as in Chicken Pancakes, p. 61, but omitting the*
> * salt and using ½ milk and ½ water for the liquid)*
> *¾ lb (350 g) curd cheese*
> *1 egg yolk*
> *2 tbsps sugar*
> *2 tbsps butter*
> *2 tbsps oil*
> *5 fl oz (150 ml) sour cream*

Make the pancakes in the usual way but leave out the salt and add ½ milk instead of all water for the batter. Fry them on one side only and set aside to cool. Mix the curd cheese with the egg yolk and sugar and put a spoonful of this filling into each blintz, cooked side up. Roll up and tuck in the ends to form small parcels and then fry them in a mixture of butter and oil for a few minutes on each side. Drain well.

Serve hot with a bowl of chilled sour cream.

❊ **Pasta Shells with Tomato Cream Sauce** ❊   (d)

1 pt ($\frac{1}{2}$ l) tomato sauce (see Kreplach, p. 58)
$\frac{3}{4}$ lb (350 g) pasta shells (or small tubes)
6 fl oz (175 ml) single cream
2 oz (50 g) grated cheese

First prepare the tomato sauce and then pass it through a sieve or blender.

Boil the pasta in plenty of salted water until it is just cooked but not too soft. Drain it and then put it into a well-buttered, ovenproof dish. Cover with the tomato sauce and then swirl in the single cream. Bake in a hot oven (gas mark 7, 425° F, 220° C) for about 15 minutes until the sauce is bubbling hot, and serve it sprinkled with grated cheese. (If you like a cooked cheese topping, add the cheese before you put it in the oven.)

❊ **Cheese and Almond Squares** ❊   (d)

8 oz (225 g) basic rich pastry (see Fish and Asparagus Flan, p. 52)
4 oz (125 g) cheese, grated
2 eggs
$2\frac{1}{2}$ fl oz (75 ml) milk
salt, cayenne pepper
2 oz (50 g) almonds, flaked and previously blanched

Make the pastry and divide it in half. Roll out one portion to fit a 10-in × 8-in (25-cm × 20-cm) tin. Press the pastry into the bottom and slightly up the sides and prick with a fork. Cover with foil and bake at gas mark 7, 425° F, 220° C for about 10 minutes, then remove the foil and continue baking for another 10 minutes to cook the base.

Meanwhile prepare the filling. Mix the cheese with the beaten eggs (reserve about 1 tsp for glazing) and add the milk, salt and a dash of cayenne pepper. The mixture should be soft but not runny. Spread it over the pastry and cover it with the other half, rolled out thinly. Mark the top into squares and scatter over the flaked almonds. Brush with the remaining beaten egg and bake in a hot oven for about 15 to 20 minutes or until the top is golden-brown. Cut the squares right through and serve them hot or cold.

❖ Borekas ❖ (d)

These little savouries are Sephardi in origin and may be filled with either spinach or cheese, but are always served hot, whichever type of pastry you choose.

CHEESE BOREKAS WITH PUFF PASTRY

3 oz (75 g) cheese, grated
2 oz (50 g) curd cheese
1 egg yolk
salt, pepper
8 oz (225 g) puff pastry

Mix together the grated cheese, curd cheese and egg yolk and season well. Roll the pastry out about $\frac{1}{8}$ in ($\frac{1}{4}$ cm) thick and cut it into 4-in (10-cm) rounds. Place a spoonful of the filling on each round, pinch the sides together to form a semicircle, and press well to enclose the cheese mixture. Bake on an ungreased tin at gas mark 7, 425° F, 220° C for about 15 minutes when the borekas will be puffed and golden and little bits of browned cheese will be oozing out.

SPINACH BOREKAS WITH PHYLLO PASTRY

This pastry is like sheets of fine paper and is available from continental delicatessens, especially Greek shops. Unlike thicker pastry, it dries very quickly so it is a good idea to cover the sheets you are not using with a damp cloth.

$\frac{1}{2}$ lb (225 g) fresh spinach
2 oz (50 g) curd cheese

1 egg yolk
salt, pepper
¼ lb (125 g) phyllo pastry
2 oz (50 g) melted butter, cooled

Cook the spinach, drain it and chop very finely. Stir in the soft cheese, egg yolk and seasoning and then leave the mixture to cool. Cut the pastry into strips about 2½ in (6 cm) wide and 8 in (20 cm) long. Put a spoonful of the spinach mixture at the end nearest to you and brush the whole strip with cooled melted butter. Then fold up the bottom corner diagonally, fold the pastry over straight, then diagonally again. Continue folding until you have reached the end of the strip, when you will be left with a triangle enclosing the filling. Brush the finished triangles with the rest of the melted butter and bake at gas mark 3, 325° F, 160° C for about 20 minutes.

❊ Corn Horns ❊   (d)

8 oz (225 g) puff pastry
4 oz (125 g) cooked sweetcorn (fresh or canned)
4 tbsps thick bechamel sauce (see Tomato Velvet Cream, p. 42)
salt, pepper

Roll out the pastry about ⅛ in (¼ cm) thick and then cut it into strips about ¾ in (2 cm) wide and 10 in (25 cm) long. Wrap these carefully round metal horn shapes and bake them in a hot oven (gas mark 7, 425° F, 220° C) for about 10 to 15 minutes until they are golden-brown and puffed.

If you do not have horn tins, make some cylinders by crushing some foil into lengths of about 4 in (10 cm) and 1 in (2½ cm) diameter. Roll out the pastry and cut it into pieces large enough to roll round them and bake as above.

When the pastry is cooked, remove the horn shapes or the tin foil and put the pastries back in the oven to cook the centres for a further five minutes.

Meanwhile, mix the bechamel sauce with the corn. Take the

pastries out of the oven. Have ready a heated dish and immediately fill each horn or cylinder with the corn mixture. Serve very hot.

5. Meat and Poultry

Traditional Jewish cooking takes no account of the fat content in many meat dishes, and for this reason many of the old favourites are frowned on today. The following tips will help to lower the calorie and cholesterol level, especially in casserole dishes, but at the same time the flavour will not suffer.

1. Wherever possible fry or sauté meat and vegetables in a non-stick pan. With fat meat or chicken, start off over low heat and the fat will begin to run out. This can then be poured away or used instead of additional fat in frying the vegetables.
2. Try to avoid using flour to thicken sauces—long slow cooking gives a delicious gravy, and cut or puréed vegetables add texture.
3. If you can, prepare the dish early in the day and pour off the sauce or gravy at least half an hour before the end of the cooking time. Refrigerate or freeze this sauce and you will then be able to remove a layer of fat from the surface. The sauce can then be poured back over the dish for the last part of the cooking time.

   Alternatively, if you are in a hurry, excess fat can be skimmed from the surface by using kitchen paper or one of the cook's brushes, especially made for absorbing grease.

BEEF
Cholent: Adafina (m)
Brisket with Chestnuts (m)
Beef and Butter Beans (m)
Charcoal-grilled Steak (m)

LAMB
Crown Roast of Lamb with Apricot Rice Stuffing (m)
Barbecued Lamb Ribs (m)
Stuffed Breast of Lamb (m)
Grandma's Stuffing for Roast Lamb or Chicken (m)

VEAL
Veal in Sherry Sauce (m)
Veal Chops (m)
Veal in White Onion Sauce (m)

CHICKEN
Spanish Chicken (m)
Chicken with Mushroom Sauce (m)
Braised Chicken with Onions (m)
Chicken with Aubergines (m)

DUCK
Glazed Duck with Cherries (m)
Duck with Apples and Honey (m)

TURKEY
Turkey Schnitzels with Lemon (m)

❊ Cholent ❊   (m)

This is a traditional dish served on the Sabbath. It is prepared the day before and left to cook very slowly all night until lunchtime the following day. There are many variations, but the essence of the dish is that it should be hot, substantial and with a rich flavour which comes from long, gentle cooking.

3 onions
½ lb (225 g) haricot or butter beans, previously soaked
3 lb (1½ kg) boneless brisket or slices of chuck steak
salt, pepper, pinch paprika
1 clove garlic, crushed
6 large potatoes, peeled or ½ lb (225 g) pearl barley

Peel the onions and cut them into quarters. In a very large, deep casserole with a well-fitting lid, place a layer of the drained, soaked beans. Then add half the onion and the brisket or slices of chuck steak. Season well and cover with the rest of the onion, crushed garlic clove and finally the whole potatoes or barley. Cover with water and bring to the boil either over heat or for about 30 minutes in a hot oven. Then cook in a very slow oven (gas mark ½, 250° F, 120° C) overnight, without uncovering. The next day there will be a rich gravy and the meat and potatoes will be a dark brown.

There is a Sephardi variation of Cholent called Adafina, in which whole eggs are added to the pot. The eggs (called hamin-das) are first boiled and then added, in their shells, to the meat casserole and cooked overnight till they are dark brown. They can be cooked separately, in which case onion skins are often added to the dish to make them a dark colour, but however they are cooked they are delicious and more digestible than ordinary hardboiled eggs. In Adafina, garbanzos or chick peas usually replace the beans and barley.

❊ Brisket with Chestnuts ❊ (m)

3–4 lb (1½–1¾ kg) rolled piece of brisket or top rib
2 onions
¾ pt (425 ml) water
1 tbsp beef fat or margarine
salt, pepper
1 lb (450 g) chestnuts

In a non-stick frying-pan brown the beef until it is seared all the way round. Remove it to a deep casserole, slice the onions and fry them in any fat which has come from the meat, adding about 1 tbsp extra if necessary. When the onions are slightly brown add them to the casserole, pour the water into the sauce-pan, stir round the pan juices and pour them into the casserole.

Season well. Then cover with a tight-fitting lid and cook at gas mark 4, 350° F, 180° C for about 2 hours.

Meanwhile, make cuts in the tops of the chestnuts, place them on a tin and put them in the oven for about 15 minutes. It will then be easier (but still not much fun!) to remove the shells.

Remove any fat from the beef gravy in the casserole and add the chestnuts for a final hour of cooking. The liquid will reduce and thicken slightly and the chestnuts will be a delicious accompaniment to the meat.

❋ Beef and Butter Beans ❋ (m)

¼ lb (125 g) butter beans
2 onions
1 tbsp beef fat or margarine
1½ lb (680 g) chuck steak
½–1 pt (¼–½ l) water
salt, pepper

Soak the butter beans overnight in cold water (or cover them with boiling water and leave for 1 hour). Slice the onions and sauté them in the fat. Transfer them to a casserole and then sauté the meat until it is brown on both sides. Add it, with the drained beans, to the onions in the casserole. Stir the pan juices with the hot water and pour this over the meat, onions and beans. Season well. Cook at gas mark 4, 350° F, 180° C for about 3 hours, checking halfway through the cooking time to see that there is enough liquid.

❋ Charcoal-grilled Steak ❋ (m)

Kosher steak often comes in for criticism as it is difficult to get the tender cuts for grilling, since these are usually from the hindquarter which is not available from kosher butchers in this country.

This way of cooking steak keeps in all the juices and adds a delicious flavour—though not, to be perfectly honest, a Jewish one! Steak is best, of course, cooked outside over charcoal, but here is the indoor recipe.

4 tbsps soy sauce
1 tsp ground ginger
1 tsp sugar
black pepper
1 clove garlic
4 short rib steaks (about 1–1½ in (2–2½ cm) thick)

Use a shallow glass dish large enough to lay out the steaks in one layer. Mix together the soy sauce, ginger, sugar and pepper with the crushed garlic clove and pour the mixture into the dish. Then put in the steaks, cover with transparent wrap and leave in the bottom of the refrigerator for about 5 hours, turning them over occasionally.

Heat the grill for about 5 minutes and place the steaks on a greased rack in the grill pan. Cook under a fierce heat for about 5 minutes and then turn them over. Brush with the remaining marinade and grill them again for 5 minutes, if you want a rare steak, 7 for medium-rare and 10 for well-done.

Serve immediately with grilled tomatoes, sauté potatoes and a sprig of watercress.

❋ Crown Roast of Lamb with Apricot Rice Stuffing ❋ (m)

4 oz (125 g) apricots, dried
8 oz (225 g) rice
1 oz (25 g) margarine
3 oz (75 g) onion, chopped
2 oz (50 g) almonds, toasted
1 tsp parsley, chopped
salt, pepper
8 lamb chops in a rack, chined

Ask the butcher to prepare the lamb chops for a 'crown roast'.

He will tie them into a circle and trim the bones, ready for roasting.

For the stuffing, soak the apricots for a few hours (or cover them with boiling water for about half an hour). Boil the rice for about 7 minutes and drain it. Melt the margarine and fry the chopped onion until it is golden. Then chop the apricots and mix them with the toasted almonds, fried onion and rice. Add the parsley and season well.

Fill the centre of the crown of lamb with the rice stuffing and cover the top with foil. Roast at gas mark 7, 425° F, 220° C for about 1 hour and then remove the foil. Carefully lift the meat on to a serving dish and decorate the tops of the bones with cutlet frills (optional).

❖ Barbecued Lamb Ribs ❖ (m)

This is an adaptation of the famous spare rib recipe using pork. There are in fact two sauces—try them both on different occasions and see which one you prefer.

For the sweet sauce
4 tbsps soy sauce
4 tbsps brown sugar
1 garlic clove, crushed
¼ pt (150 ml) water
1 beef stock cube
½ tsp ground ginger
3 tbsps sherry

For the barbecue sauce
4 tbsps tomato purée
1 tsp barbecue spice
juice of ½ lemon
2 tbsps soft brown sugar
¼ pt (150 ml) tomato juice
salt, pepper

In both cases use one large breast of lamb per person.

Cut as much fat as possible off the breasts of lamb and then cut them downwards into ribs, placing these on a rack over a grill pan. Roast them in a preheated oven (gas mark 7, 425° F, 220° C) for about 30 minutes, by which time some of the remaining fat should have melted into the pan. Remove the ribs to an ovenproof dish while you prepare the sauce.

For the sweet sauce, boil all the ingredients together for 5 minutes. For the barbecue sauce, just mix everything together in a bowl. Then pour the sauce you have chosen over the lamb ribs and continue cooking them for a further 30 minutes in a lower oven (gas mark 4, 350° F, 180° C). When they are cooked the ribs will be slightly sticky and are delicious served with rice, noodles or home-made baked beans (see Boston Baked Beans, p. 89).

The lamb ribs can, of course, be cooked on an open barbecue over charcoal, in which case just baste them continually with the sauce, cooking them for about 30 to 40 minutes altogether.

❊ Stuffed Breast of Lamb ❊   (m)

3 large breasts of lamb, boned
2 medium-sized onions, chopped
$\frac{1}{2}$ oz (15 g) beef fat or margarine
2 fl oz (50 ml) water
4 oz (125 g) fresh breadcrumbs
2 tbsps parsley, chopped
salt, pepper

Trim off as much fat as possible from the breasts of lamb and then flatten them slightly with a rolling pin.

To make the stuffing, sauté the chopped onions in the fat until they are golden-brown. Add the water and cook over high heat for a few minutes. Pour the onions and the slightly reduced liquid over the breadcrumbs and chopped parsley and mix well. Season to taste and spread the stuffing over the breasts of lamb. Roll them up and tie with string.

Roast the stuffed lamb in an ungreased tin in a preheated hot oven (gas mark 7, 425° F, 220° C) for about 15 minutes. Turn the heat down to gas mark 5, 375° F, 190° C and continue roasting for about an hour or until the lamb is tender. Pour away any fat and remove the meat to a serving dish. De-glaze the pan with a little stock or water to make the gravy and serve the lamb with roast potatoes. (These may be cooked in the oven at the same time as the meat.)

Note : for Stuffed Breast of Veal, make the stuffing in the same way and spread it in the pocket of a boned breast of veal (about 2¾ lb (1¼ kg) boned weight). Melt ½ oz (15 g) fat in a roasting dish and cook the veal for about 2 hours in a fairly slow oven (gas mark 4, 350° F, 180° C).

�֍ Grandma's Stuffing for Roast Lamb or Chicken �֍ (m)

Here is an alternative stuffing which can be used with any roast meat. It definitely has a Scottish-Jewish origin!

2 oz (50 g) unrendered chicken fat
1 medium-sized Spanish onion, grated
2 oz (50 g) matzo meal, medium-ground
2 oz (50 g) porridge oats (uncooked)
¾ tsp mixed spice
salt, pepper
warm water to bind

Chop the chicken fat (which can be taken from a cleaned, prepared chicken) into small pieces. Then mix it, with the grated onion, into the dry ingredients. Season well with salt, pepper and spice and add enough warm water to bind the mixture together—it should not be soft or sticky. Use the stuffing for chicken, lamb or veal and roast in the usual way, or use it in the traditional way as filling for stuffed neck (helzel).

❖ Veal in Sherry Sauce ❖ (m)

This is very similar to the Italian *scallopine alla marsala*, but the wine used in this version is kosher sherry which gives a very good taste.

> $1\frac{1}{4}$ *lb* (575 g) *thin veal cutlets, beaten flat*
> 4 *tbsps flour*
> *salt, pepper*
> *oil for frying*
> $\frac{1}{4}$ *pt* (150 ml) *sherry*

Beat the cutlets until they are very thin and dry them well. Toss them in seasoned flour and fry them in a few tablespoons of very hot oil in a shallow pan. Turn them over after a few minutes to brown the other side and then pour over the sherry, turning up the heat to reduce the sauce. When it is bubbling, stir in all the pan juices, season well and transfer to a serving dish. The cutlets will keep warm for up to half an hour, but make sure they are covered so that the sauce does not dry up.

❖ Veal Chops ❖ (m)

This recipe has no title since we always refer to it at home as 'veal with gnomes' goulash' as the vegetables are cut into such tiny pieces. It is quick and easy and tastes as if it is more complicated!

> 1 *carrot*
> 1 *stick celery*
> 1 *onion*
> 5 *tbsps oil or margarine*
> 4 *veal chops*
> 8 *fl oz* (225 ml) *sherry*
> 1 *tbsp tomato purée*
> *salt, pepper*
> 1 *tbsp parsley, chopped*

Chop the carrot, celery and onion into very small pieces and sauté them in a little oil or margarine until they are golden. Continue cooking for about 10 minutes over low heat until they are soft and then transfer them to a heated dish while you cook the chops.

Pour the rest of the oil into the pan and fry the chops over high heat for about 7 minutes on each side until they are brown. Mix the sherry with the tomato purée and pour it over the chops. Add the chopped vegetables, season well, and boil briskly for a few minutes. Remove the chops to a serving dish, garnish with the chopped vegetables, cover with the sauce and sprinkle over the parsley.

❖ Veal in White Onion Sauce ❖   (m)

The delicately flavoured onion sauce is suitable for chicken and turkey too—and it is very slimming!

4 veal chops
3 large onions
1 pt ($\frac{1}{2}$ l) veal or chicken stock
2 tbsps chicken fat or margarine
salt, pepper

Sauté the veal chops in a little fat in a large frying-pan and cook them for about 5 minutes each side, when they will be lightly coloured. Transfer them to a shallow ovenproof dish. Slice the onions thickly and cook them briefly in the frying-pan in any fat that remains and then pour over the veal or chicken stock. Bring to the boil, stir in the pan juices, cover and simmer until the onions are very soft. Then pass the cooked onions through a sieve or blender and pour the onion purée sauce over the chops. Season well, cover and cook in a moderate oven (gas mark 4, 350° F, 180° C) for about 40 minutes or until the chops are tender.

Serve with creamed potatoes or rice and a dark green vegetable like broccoli or beans.

❖ Spanish Chicken ❖ (m)

This dish has the real flavour of sun-ripened peppers and tomatoes and is a traditional way of cooking chicken among Sephardi
Jews.

> *1 large (5-lb (2-kg)) chicken, jointed*
> *2 large red peppers, de-seeded and sliced*
> *1 onion, sliced*
> *1 clove garlic, crushed*
> *oil for frying*
> *3 ripe tomatoes, peeled*
> *1 tbsp water*
> *1 tsp sugar*
> *salt, pepper*

Sauté the chicken joints in a non-stick frying-pan until some
of the fat begins to run and the skin starts to brown. Remove
them to an ovenproof dish or casserole. Fry the peppers, onion
and garlic in the fat remaining in the pan, adding a little oil if
necessary. Smother the chicken with the peppers and onions
and then add the chopped tomatoes to the pan with a little
water and sugar. Stir over heat for a few minutes, season and
then pour the tomato mixture into the dish. Cook, covered, for
about an hour at gas mark 5, 375° F, 190° C.

Serve hot with white rice.

❖ Chicken with Mushroom Sauce ❖ (m)

> *1 5-lb (2-kg) boiling chicken*
> *1 carrot*
> *1 onion*
> *salt, pepper*
> *3 tbsps flour*
> *8 oz (225 g) button mushrooms, chopped*

Place the chicken in a deep saucepan with the carrot, onion and seasoning and cook as for Chicken Soup (p. 37) until it is very tender. Then remove the chicken from the soup, strain the liquid and take off the fat.

Cut the chicken into large pieces (removing the skin) and keep these warm in an ovenproof dish while you make the sauce.

Make a chicken sauce with 1 oz (25 g) of the chicken fat, the flour and $\frac{3}{4}$ pt of the chicken stock (see Chicken Soufflé, p. 30). Sauté the mushrooms in a little more fat and add these to the chicken sauce together with the brown juices. Stir well and pour the sauce over the chicken.

Serve hot with mashed or jacket potatoes, or alternatively use as a filling for pancakes.

❈ Braised Chicken with Onions ❈ (m)

Start this dish early in the day or the day before it is to be served, and use a very large boiling chicken.

> *1 6-lb (3-kg) boiling chicken, very well cleaned*
> *2 large Spanish onions, sliced*
> *salt, pepper*

Prick the skin of the chicken and place it in a non-stick pan over medium heat. Turn it around and cook it gently for about 10 minutes until some of the fat has run out and the skin is starting to brown all over. Remove the chicken to a casserole with a tight-fitting lid or a large saucepan. In the fat, sauté the onions until they are golden-brown and then put them all round and over the chicken. Season very well and then deglaze the pan with about $\frac{1}{2}$ pt of hot water, pour it over the chicken in the pot and top it up with more water until it is about 2 in (5 cm) deep. Bring to the boil and then simmer it slowly, either on low heat or in a slow oven (gas mark 4, 350° F, 180° C) for about 3 hours. Remove the fat.

Serve the chicken carved into portions with plenty of browned onions.

❄ Chicken with Aubergines ❄   (m)

This is similar to Spanish Chicken, but in this dish the chicken is roasted first and the sauce is prepared separately.

>   *1 5-lb (2-kg) roasting chicken*
>   *5 large tomatoes, peeled and chopped*
>   *1 clove garlic, crushed*
>   *2 aubergines, peeled and cubed*
>   *2 onions, sliced*
>   *2 tbsps oil*
>   *3 fl oz (75 ml) dry white wine*
>   *salt, pepper, sugar*

Roast the chicken in a hot oven (gas mark 7, 425° F, 220° C) for about an hour. After about 30 minutes add the tomatoes and garlic and baste the chicken with this mixture.

While it is cooking prepare the aubergines. Leave them covered with salt in a colander for about half an hour. Then wash, drain and pat them dry to get rid of any bitter juices. Sauté the onion and the aubergine pieces in the oil until they are crisp and brown.

When the chicken is cooked, carve it into portions. Pour off any fat from the pan juices and stir in the wine. Season to taste, add a little sugar and then sieve the sauce over the chicken. Cover with the hot sautéed aubergine and onion.

❄ Glazed Duck with Cherries ❄   (m)

Duck, though not particularly Jewish, has now taken the place of chicken as a special occasion dish. This one is good in summer as it can be prepared well in advance and looks attractive.

>   *1 5-lb (2-kg) duck, with the giblets*
>   *3 tbsps redcurrant jelly*
>   *2 tbsps lemon juice*
>   *salt, pepper*

For the garnish

*8 oz (225 g) canned or fresh cherries, poached in water for 5
   minutes*

2 small oranges

1 bunch watercress

Prick the skin of the duck and roast in a hot oven (gas mark 7,
425° F, 220° C) for about 1¼ to 1½ hours, frequently pouring off
the fat which will be released from underneath the skin. (This
is especially important as the duck should not be at all greasy
when served cold.) While it is cooking simmer the giblets in
water to make a broth for the glaze.

When the duck is cooked, leave it to get cold and then carve
it into serving portions. Strain ¼ pt (150 ml) giblet broth into a
saucepan, add the redcurrant jelly and lemon juice and ¼ pt
(150 ml) cherry juice, and season to taste. Boil briskly until the
jelly is completely dissolved and the mixture coats the back of
a spoon. With tissues, blot any remaining fat from the surface
of the duck and then coat it with the glaze.

With a sharp-pointed knife, cut the oranges into halves or
basket shapes. Take out the orange flesh and fill the baskets
with the drained cherries. Place the duck on a serving dish and
garnish it with sprigs of watercress and the orange and cherry
baskets.

Serve cold with a salad of new potatoes and cooked summer
vegetables.

❖ Duck with Apples and Honey ❖ (m)

1 5–6-lb (2–3-kg) duck, with the giblets

1 tbsp clear honey

¼ pt (150 ml) dry red wine

½ pt (¼ l) duck stock

salt, pepper

3 oz (75 g) margarine

2 large cooking apples, peeled and quartered

  2 tbsps soft brown sugar
  1 lb (450 g) baby onions, peeled

First make a stock by simmering the giblets in water for about
an hour.

Cut the duck into four portions and prick the skin well. Then
sauté it in a non-stick pan over low heat at first, until the fat
begins to run from underneath the skin. Add the honey and
continue cooking until the duck is crisp and brown, and then
transfer the joints to a casserole. Pour the red wine and ½ pt (¼ l)
stock into the pan juices and stir well. Season and pour over
the duck and cook in a moderate oven (gas mark 4, 350° F,
180° C) for about 1 hour, or until it is tender.

Meanwhile, melt the margarine and use some of it to paint
the apple quarters. Place these on a greased baking sheet,
sprinkle them with a little sugar and cook on a shelf above the
duck for about 20 minutes.

Sauté the baby onions in the rest of the margarine until they
start to brown. Then add the rest of the brown sugar and shake
over moderate heat until they are slightly caramelized. This
will take about 15 minutes.

Remove any fat from the gravy, reduce it slightly over high
heat, check seasoning and then serve it in a separate sauce-boat,
reserving a little to pour over the duck quarters, garnished with
apples and onions.

❖ Turkey Schnitzels with Lemon ❖   (m)

This is a very popular dish in Israel and in this country too, as
the veal called for in the original recipe is so expensive.

  1½ lb (680 g) turkey slices, cut very thin from the breast
  2 tbsps flour
  salt, pepper
  3 eggs
  8 oz (225 g) matzo meal, medium-ground
  oil for frying

For the garnish
lemon quarters

Pound the slices until they are very thin and then toss them in
seasoned flour. Beat the eggs well and dip the turkey first in the
beaten egg and then in the matzo meal.

In a shallow pan fry the schnitzels in a single layer in very hot
oil for about 5 minutes on each side, or until they are golden-
brown. Put them on a serving dish in a warm oven until you
have finished frying them all.

Garnish the dish with lemon quarters and serve with sauté
potatoes or rice.

6. Vegetables and Salads

Eastern European communities were rather restricted in their vegetables, so beans, lentils and potatoes formed a large part of their diet. In the Middle East and Spain, peppers, aubergines, rice and stuffed vegetables of all types have always been favourites.

In England we are lucky enough to have an enormous choice of fresh salads and vegetables from the beginning of spring until the autumn. There are young carrots, broad beans, new potatoes and peas (and also the more expensive asparagus and artichokes). All these need very little cooking, and even the winter cauliflower, broccoli, leeks and celery need only very little water and light cooking to make them appetizing. In my selection I concentrate on some more imaginative combinations which I hope will be new to some of you.

HOT
Portuguese Rice (m)
Boston Baked Beans (m)
Stir-fried Cabbage and Bean Sprouts (m)
Chestnuts and Artichokes (p)
Potato Nests (p)
Tomatoes with Garlic Crumb Stuffing (p)

COLD
Frankfurters and Potato Salad (m)
Baby Onions in Spicy Tomato Sauce (p)
Celeriac Salad (p)
Red Pepper Salad (p)
Rice Salad (p)
Sliced Aubergine Salad (p)

Crunchy Winter Salad (p)
Cucumbers in Sour Cream (d)
Harlequin Peppers (d)

❊ **Portuguese Rice** ❊ (m)

8 oz (225 g) rice
1 Spanish onion, chopped
1 clove garlic (optional)
2 tbsps oil
1–1¼ pt (550–700 ml) beef stock
1 tbsp tomato purée

Soak the rice in hot water in a bowl for about 5 minutes, then drain off the white starchy liquid.

Sauté the onion and garlic in the oil for a few minutes and then add the rice, stirring until all the grains are coated with oil. Add the beef stock and tomato purée and bring to the boil. Stir once, brushing any grains of rice that stick to the side of the pan into the stock, then cover and simmer over low heat for about 15 minutes. Taste for seasoning and add a little more stock or water if the rice is still a bit firm and the stock has been completely absorbed. When the rice is cooked, turn it into a bowl and fluff it up with a fork.

❊ **Boston Baked Beans** ❊ (m)

I include this old New England recipe because it has an interesting history. The American version (which always contained salt pork) was prepared on the Saturday and left to cook in a slow oven so that it would be ready for Sunday dinner—an early New World manifestation of Sabbath Day observance!

¾ lb (350 g) haricot beans
½ pt (¼ l) tomato juice

2 heaped tbsps golden syrup
1 tbsp tomato purée
½ tsp salt
1 beef stock cube, crumbled
pepper

Soak the beans in water overnight or cover them with boiling water and leave for a few hours. Then either cook for about 20 minutes in a pressure cooker, or for about an hour in a normal saucepan, and test to see that they are done—they should be just soft. Transfer them with some of the cooking juice to a casserole and add all the other ingredients. Cover and cook at gas mark ½, 250° F, 120° C for 2 to 3 hours or until the beans have absorbed the rich liquid and are almost sticky.

Serve with barbecued lamb or viennas (see Glossary).

❈ Stir-fried Cabbage and Bean Sprouts ❈ (m)

1 tbsp oil
1 onion, thinly sliced
4 oz (125 g) cabbage, shredded
9 oz (250 g) bean sprouts
1 beef stock cube
2 tbsps soy sauce

In a heavy, deep frying-pan heat the oil and sauté the onion quickly. When it is just turning brown, add the shredded cabbage and the bean sprouts and stir-fry for a few moments. Crumble the cube very finely and add it with the soy sauce to the mixture. Continue stirring until well mixed and serve immediately. The vegetables should not be stewed but should stay crisp.

Serve with roast or grilled meats.

❖ Chestnuts and Artichokes ❖ (p)

An alternative to stuffing with roast meats, these can be prepared in advance and frozen.

> ½ *lb* (*225 g*) *chestnut purée, tinned and unsweetened or ½ lb*
>   (*225 g*) *purée made from fresh chestnuts*
> *salt, pepper*
> *1 14-oz* (*400-g*) *can artichoke hearts*

Mix the chestnut purée with salt and pepper to taste and then
put the mixture into a forcing bag. Remove the hairy centre
from the artichoke hearts and then pipe the chestnut mixture
in rosettes on to each one. Heat through for about 15 minutes
in a hot oven (gas mark 7, 425° F, 220° C).

Serve the stuffed artichokes round a joint of veal or chicken.

❖ Potato Nests ❖ (p)

> 2½ *lb* (*1 kg*) *potatoes*
> 1½ *oz* (*40 g*) *margarine*
> *1 tbsp parev 'milk' powder*
> *salt, pepper*
> *1 egg yolk*

> For serving
> *mixed vegetables, peas or beans*

Peel the potatoes and cut them into small pieces. Cook in
salted water for about 10 minutes until they are soft. Then drain
them very well and return them to the pan over low heat for a
few minutes to make sure they are very dry. Add the margarine,
parev 'milk' powder and seasoning and mash them very well,
making sure there are no lumps. Finally, mix in the egg yolk.

With a forcing bag, pipe circles of the potato mixture on to a
greased baking sheet. Pipe round the circles again and build up
the outsides to make 'nests'. This amount will make about 9

2½-in (7-cm) nests. They can be made in advance and heated through in the oven just before serving, when they should be filled with mixed vegetables, peas or beans.

❖ Tomatoes with Garlic Crumb Stuffing ❖ (p)

1 lb (450 g) large ripe tomatoes
2 cloves garlic, crushed
1 oz (25 g) fresh breadcrumbs
1 oz (25 g) parsley, chopped
salt, pepper
3 tsps olive oil

Cut the tomatoes in half and make a few slashes in the flesh. Mix together the crushed garlic, breadcrumbs, parsley and seasoning and press the mixture well into each tomato. Dot with a little olive oil and grill for about 15 to 20 minutes, when they will be well done and even a little charred. Warning—if you prepare this in advance, everything in the kitchen will smell of garlic!

❖ Frankfurters and Potato Salad ❖ (m)

1¼ lb (575 g) potatoes
4 oz (125 g) frankfurters, cooked and sliced
¼ pt (150 ml) mayonnaise
paprika

To make the potato salad, cut the raw potatoes into cubes first and then boil them in salted water for about 10 minutes. This prevents their collapsing or going floury. When the potatoes are cool, add the frankfurters and mix together with the mayonnaise. Pile into a bowl and sprinkle with paprika.

❖ Baby Onions in Spicy Tomato Sauce ❖ (p)

These onions are very good with hot fresh bread as a starter or as a side dish with cold meat or chicken. You can make them well in advance as they keep for several days in the refrigerator.

36 baby onions, peeled
10 fl oz (300 ml) dry white wine
6 fl oz (160 ml) olive oil
1 tbsp wine vinegar
1 bay leaf
1 garlic clove, crushed
salt, pepper
2 tbsps tomato purée
4 oz (125 g) sultanas

Place the onions with the wine, oil, wine vinegar, bay leaf, garlic and seasoning in a heavy saucepan and bring to the boil. Simmer until the onions are tender and then stir in the tomato purée and the sultanas. Leave to cool.

❖ Celeriac Salad ❖ (p)

10 oz (275 g) celeriac
4 oz (125 g) canned artichoke hearts, chopped
2 large tomatoes, peeled and chopped
1 russet apple, chopped
oil, lemon juice

Cut the celeriac into strips and blanch for 1 minute in boiling salted water. Drain well and then add the artichoke hearts, tomatoes and apple. Mix some oil and lemon juice to taste and moisten the salad with this dressing.

❖ Red Pepper Salad ❖ (p)

The flavour of ripe, red peppers is the essence of this salad. Serve it with cold meats or fish, or with a crisp wedge of lettuce as a starter to a meal.

> *2 small onions, thinly sliced*
> *olive oil for frying*
> *3 red peppers, de-seeded and thinly sliced*
> *5 ripe tomatoes, peeled and roughly chopped*
> *2 cloves garlic, crushed*
> *salt, pepper*
> *1½ tsps sugar*

Sauté the onions in a little olive oil in a frying-pan. When they are soft but not brown, add the peppers and cook for another few minutes. Then add the tomatoes, garlic and seasoning. Cover and cook for about 10 minutes and leave to cool before serving.

❖ Rice Salad ❖ (p)

A good winter salad which makes a change from the better-known celery and apple combination.

> *1 lb (450 g) rice, cooked*
> *4 oz (125 g) peas, cooked*
> *1 large red apple, chopped*
> *4 oz (125 g) celery, chopped*
> *1 oz (25 g) sultanas*

> For the dressing
> *1 tsp honey*
> *1 tbsp lemon juice*
> *1 tsp curry powder*
> *3 tbsps olive oil*
> *salt, pepper*

Mix together the cooked rice and peas and add the chopped apple, celery and sultanas. Melt the honey if it is very thick and stir in the lemon juice, curry powder and oil. Season to taste and add just enough of the dressing to moisten the rice mixture, turn it over well and pile up in a bowl.

❖ Sliced Aubergine Salad ❖   (p)

An unusual method of cooking aubergines, which tend to absorb very large amounts of oil when fried.

> *2 large aubergines*
> *salt, pepper*
> *5 tbsps water*
> *2 tsps tomato purée*
> *2 tsps sugar*
> *2 cloves garlic, crushed*
> *sprinkling dried mixed herbs*
> *2 tbsps olive oil*

Cut the aubergines into ½-in (1½-cm) slices and sprinkle with salt. Place them in a colander and leave to drain for about half an hour to remove the bitter juices. Wash and pat dry and then place the slices in a greased, ovenproof dish. Cover them with a mixture of water, tomato purée, sugar, garlic, salt, pepper and mixed herbs to taste and dot all over with the olive oil. Bake at gas mark 5, 375° F, 190° C for about 30 to 40 minutes or until the aubergine slices are soft.

Serve either hot as a vegetable or cold as a salad.

❖ Crunchy Winter Salad ❖   (p)

This is a delicious variation on the well-known cole slaw and is a good combination of crunchy and soft textures.

> *½ small celeriac, peeled*
> *¼ white cabbage*

½ *cucumber, peeled*
½ *lb (225 g) french beans, cooked*
1 chinese radish (or several small ones)
¼ *pt (125 ml) mayonnaise*
salt, pepper

Cut the celeriac into strips and blanch them in boiling water for a minute. Drain and rinse in cold water. Shred the cabbage, dice the cucumber and mix together with the beans and celeriac strips. Add some slices of radish and fold in the mayonnaise. Season to taste.

Pile the salad into a bowl and decorate the edges with circles of radish and a few slices of cucumber.

❖ Cucumbers in Sour Cream ❖ (d)

1 large cucumber, peeled
salt, pepper
6 fl oz (175 ml) sour cream (or smatana)
1 tbsp fresh mint leaves, chopped

Slice the cucumber thinly and sprinkle with plenty of salt. Leave in a colander for at least an hour to drain. Remove any excess salt and pat the slices dry with kitchen paper. Place the slices in a shallow serving dish, season and cover with the sour cream or smatana.

Garnish with chopped mint leaves and serve chilled.

❖ Harlequin Peppers ❖ (d)

These are very attractive on individual salad plates or as part of a buffet.

3 red, green or orange peppers
12 oz (350 g) cream cheese
9 radishes, finely diced

9 *spring onions, finely diced*
½ *cucumber, finely diced*

Remove the tops from the peppers and take out the seeds and membrane from the centres. Wash and dry them very well. Mix the cream cheese with the radishes, spring onions, cucumber and diced pepper tops. Press the mixture firmly back into the peppers and leave in the refrigerator to chill for several hours. Then with a sharp knife, dipped in hot water, cut the peppers horizontally into slices and arrange them on a dish.

7. Desserts

Our grandmothers would probably have ended the meal with a glass of lemon tea, some stewed fruit and a slice of plava (sponge cake) or kugel (pudding). We have become more adventurous and instead of apple pie, we want to try something new. But this often presents a problem with the ingredients, so with the desserts and gâteaux I have concentrated mainly on non-dairy sweets which may be served after a meat meal.

One of the best ways to end a meal, either as an accompaniment to a dessert or on its own, is with a selection of fresh fruit. This can be presented either as a fruit salad using a combination of up to ten or twelve different fruits in season, or more simply as a platter of one or two complementary fruits, such as pineapple and black grapes, or slices of melon and cherries.

Pancakes (p)
Pear and Walnut Tart with Chocolate Sauce (p)
Fijuelas (p)
Sherry Custard (p)
Parev Ice Cream (p)
Chocolate Alaska (p)
Lemon Mousse (p)
Orange Charlotte (p)
Chocolate Mousse (p) Chocolate Rum Cream (d)
Cream Cheese Crêpes with Apricot Sauce (d)
Lockshen Pudding (d)
Caramel Mousse (d)
Iced Apricot Mousse (d) or (p)
Black Cherry Roll (d)

❊ **Pancakes** ❊ (p)

4 oz (125 g) plain flour
pinch salt
1 egg, beaten
¼ pt (150 ml) orange juice, fresh or frozen
¼ pt (150 ml) iced water
oil for frying

Mix together the flour and salt in a large bowl. Make a well in the centre and gradually add the beaten egg, orange juice and water, stirring well to avoid lumps. (If you have a blender, put everything in together and liquidize for a few seconds to make the batter.)

Put about a tablespoon of oil in a small frying-pan and heat it. Then pour it back into a small jug, leaving just a film of oil, and pour some of the batter into the pan. Turn it round quickly to coat the base of the pan and with a palette knife loosen the edges from the sides of the pan, as the pancake cooks. Turn the pancake over and cook for a few more minutes on the other side. Continue until all the batter is used up. This amount will make about 12 pancakes of 6-in (15-cm) diameter. To store them, stack each one with a layer of greaseproof paper between them and either freeze or keep in the refrigerator for up to a week.

To reheat the pancakes, either steam them over a pan of simmering water, or place in a covered dish in the oven, until they are heated through.

Suggested pancake fillings
cooked sliced apples topped with cinnamon sugar
mincemeat with brandy-flavoured ice-cream
whole chestnuts with hot, flambéed chocolate liqueur
whole or sliced bananas with lemon juice and sugar
fresh peaches topped with raspberry purée
strawberries with vanilla sugar

Heat the plates and make sure the pancakes are really hot. Have

the filling you have chosen ready and assemble them quickly.
Serve the pancakes immediately.

❊ Pear and Walnut Tart with Chocolate Sauce ❊ (p)

For the pastry
5 oz (150 g) margarine
12 oz (350 g) plain flour
4 oz (125 g) caster sugar
1 tsp cinnamon
3 oz (75 g) walnuts, finely chopped
3 egg yolks
1½ tsps iced water
1 egg white

For the filling
4 large pears

For the sauce
8 oz (225 g) chocolate
2 tbsps golden syrup
1½ oz (40 g) margarine
6 tbsps water

To make the pastry, rub the margarine into the flour and add
3 oz (75 g) of the sugar, the cinnamon and the chopped nuts.
Mix to a dough with the beaten egg yolks and iced water and
leave to chill for 30 minutes.

Roll out the pastry and line an 8-in (20-cm) pie dish with
half of it. Fill with the peeled, sliced pears and cover with the
rest of the pastry. Brush with beaten egg white and sprinkle
with the rest of the sugar. Bake at gas mark 4, 350° F, 180° C
for 35 minutes.

Melt the chocolate, syrup and margarine in a heavy saucepan
over low heat and add the water. Stir to make a thick, dark sauce.

When the tart is cooked serve it hot with the chocolate sauce
in a separate sauce-boat.

❈ Fijuelas ❈ (p)

This is a Portuguese dessert, traditionally eaten after the fast on the Day of Atonement. Fijuelas are crisp, fried pastry coils, soaked in sweet syrup.

2 eggs
1 tbsp orange flower water
1 tbsp olive oil
pinch salt
3 tbsps cold water
9 oz (250 g) plain flour
oil for frying

For the syrup
8 oz (225 g) granulated sugar
10 fl oz ($\frac{1}{4}$ l) water
1 tsp cinnamon

Beat together the eggs, orange flower water, oil and salt. Then add the water and enough flour to make a soft, pliable dough. Knead it very well and roll it out into two *very thin* pieces. Cut into strips about 8 in (20 cm) long and 2 in (5 cm) wide.

Have ready a pan half full of hot oil and taking one end of each strip, carefully lower it into the oil. As it touches the oil, turn it slowly with a long-handled fork until it forms a coil, turning it over and over in the hot oil to fry each part of it. Remove the fork and continue frying until each roll is golden-brown, and then drain well. When all the strips are used up, arrange the coils in a bowl.

For the syrup, bring the sugar and water to the boil and then add the cinnamon. Pour the hot syrup over the fijuelas and leave them to cool.

❊ Sherry Custard ❊ (p)

Very like the Italian zabaglione made with marsala, this custard is delicious hot or cold. You can either serve it in glasses or pour it over fruit or sponge cake.

4 egg yolks
4 tbsps caster sugar
4 tbsps sweet sherry

Whisk the egg yolks with the sugar until they are thick and pale. Then put the bowl over a pan of simmering water and continue whisking over heat while you add the sherry. (You actually need three hands for this operation!) As you continue to whisk, the mixture will darken slightly and become thick. Serve it immediately—although it is good cold it will probably separate.

❊ Parev Ice Cream ❊ (p)

Nothing replaces the flavour of fresh dairy cream. However, if you want to serve ice cream after a meat meal, using the parev whip can be successful if you add it to a strong basic flavour, and an added advantage is that the texture will be softer. The basic mixture may be adapted to many different flavourings, but remember that freezing often dulls both strength and sweetness.

For the ice cream
4 large eggs
4 oz (125 g) caster sugar
$\frac{1}{2}$ *pt ($\frac{1}{4}$ l) parev whip*

For the flavourings
3 large bananas, mashed or 3 large fresh peaches, mashed or $\frac{1}{2}$ lb (225 g) strawberries, mashed or 4 oz (125 g) praline (see Praline Creams, p. 157) or 2 tbsps strong coffee or 2 tbsps cocoa powder mixed with 1 tbsp boiling water or 2 tbsps raisins, soaked in rum overnight

To make the ice cream, whisk the eggs with the sugar in a bowl until they are very light, almost white and fluffy. In another bowl whisk the parev whip until it is thick. Fold together the eggs, whip and whatever flavouring or fruit purée you are using, and freeze for about 1 hour. Take out the ice cream, stir it well and refreeze for a further 2 hours or until it is firm. This ice cream should be taken out of the freezer and left in the refrigerator for about 15 minutes before serving. (The fruit purée ice creams are slightly harder due to the higher water content.)

❖ Chocolate Alaska ❖ (p)

From the title you can guess just how Jewish this recipe is! However, my excuse for including it, apart from the fact that it is delicious, is that I adapted it from the well-known version as a good party dessert to serve after a meat meal.

1 8-in (20-cm) sponge cake round (see Light Sponge Cake, p. 112)
½ pt (¼ l) parev chocolate ice cream (see previous recipe)
4 pears, cooked and drained
3 egg whites
3 oz (75 g) caster sugar

Place the sponge round in an ovenproof dish or tin of the same size. Spread the very hard chocolate ice cream over the cake and arrange the halved, cooked pears on top. Put the dish back in the freezer or refrigerator while you prepare the meringue.

Preheat the oven to gas mark 6, 400° F, 200° C. Whisk the egg whites until they are very stiff and then fold in the sugar until the mixture is firm enough to stay in the bowl if it is held upside down. Pipe the mixture over the pears, making sure that every bit is completely covered, and immediately put the dish into the oven for 5 to 10 minutes. The meringue will be hot, but soft, and the pears and ice cream will be deliciously cool, but you must serve it straight away or the ice cream will melt.

Note : the amount of sugar is less than for normal meringue as the combination of cake and ice cream is already very sweet.

❖ Lemon Mousse ❖   (p)

The joy of this dessert is its fresh-tasting lightness. Success
depends on the careful use of gelatin, so please refer to the
notes in the recipe for Melon with Fresh Orange Jelly, p. 32,
first.

> *1 tbsp kosher gelatin*
> *the juice and grated rind of 4 lemons*
> *6 large eggs, separated*
> *6 oz (175 g) caster sugar*

> For decoration
> *grapes, orange segments or cubed pineapple*

First prepare the gelatin with some of the lemon juice. Whisk
the egg yolks with the sugar and grated lemon rind until the
mixture is pale and thick. Then in a double saucepan, or in a
pan over simmering water, stir the lemon juice into the mixture
and keep stirring until it thickens—this will take about 5
minutes. Thoroughly stir in the warm gelatin mixture and
remove from the heat. Leave to cool and then whisk the whites of
egg until they are stiff. Fold quickly and carefully into the cold
lemon mixture and spoon into a glass bowl.

Chill for several hours and then decorate with grapes, orange
segments or pineapple.

Note : the mousse can be made in the same way with oranges,
using slightly less sugar, i.e. $5\frac{1}{2}$ oz (160 g) and 4 small oranges and
$\frac{1}{2}$ lemon.

❖ Orange Charlotte ❖   (p)

This is a combination of two recipes (Orange Mousse, see note
to previous recipe, and Light Sponge Cake, p. 112). It can be
made the day before and looks elegant when turned out.

For the sponge cake lining
3 eggs
3 oz (75 g) caster sugar
3 oz (75 g) self-raising flour
grated rind of 1 orange

For the mousse filling
3 eggs
3 tsps gelatin
rind and juice of 3 oranges and ½ lemon
1 tsp orange liqueur

For decoration
grapes or mandarin oranges

First make the sponge cake base (see Light Sponge Cake, p. 112) and add the grated orange rind when folding in the flour. Use the mixture to make one 8-in (20-cm) sandwich layer and pipe the rest on to a baking sheet to make sponge fingers. Bake for about 10 minutes and leave to cool.

Meanwhile, make the mousse (see note to previous recipe). Reserve a few spoonfuls of the orange juice and add to the orange liqueur. When the cake is cool, cut the sponge sandwich in half, making two very thin layers, and place one layer on the bottom of a cake tin of identical size (preferably with a loose base). Put the sponge fingers around the inside of the tin (leaving a small gap in between each if there are not enough to go all the way round). Brush the cake with the orange liqueur mixture and gently pour in half of the orange mousse mixture. Lay the second layer of sponge cake on top of the mousse and cover it completely with the rest of the mixture. Smooth it out and chill well.

To serve the dessert, remove it carefully from the tin and decorate it with grapes or fresh mandarin oranges.

❁ Chocolate Mouse ❁ (p)

6 eggs, separated
9 oz (250 g) plain chocolate

Put the egg yolks into a bowl. In a double saucepan (or in another bowl set over simmering water) melt the chocolate, making sure that no water spills into it. When it is melted, add it quickly to the egg yolks, stirring all the time. Leave to cool. Whisk the egg whites until they are stiff but not too dry and then fold them in quickly but carefully with the chocolate mixture. Be careful that there are no lumps of egg white but do not go on stirring too much as the mousse will lose its lightness if you do.

Pile the mixture into a bowl and refrigerate for a few hours.

Note : to make Chocolate Rum Cream, add 2 tbsps rum or other liqueur to the yolks and melted chocolate mixture. Leave to cool as above. Then fold in the whisked egg whites together with $\frac{1}{4}$ pt (150 ml) whipped cream, reserving a little cream for decoration.

❆ Cream Cheese Crêpes with Apricot Sauce ❆   (d)

12 pancakes (see Pancakes, p. 99, but use $\frac{1}{2}$ pt ($\frac{1}{4}$ l) milk for liquid)
8 oz (225 g) cream cheese, softened
2 oz (50 g) butter, softened
2 oz (50 g) caster sugar
$1\frac{1}{2}$ tsps vanilla essence

For the sauce
3 tbsps apricot jam
juice of $\frac{1}{2}$ orange
juice of $\frac{1}{2}$ lemon
grated rind of 1 orange and 1 lemon

First make the pancakes, using cold milk instead of the water and orange juice in the Pancakes recipe on p. 99. Mix together the cream cheese, butter, sugar and vanilla essence and spread the pancakes with the mixture. Fold in the ends and roll over to make little parcels, making sure the filling is completely enclosed. Arrange them in a shallow, buttered ovenproof dish and bake for 10 minutes at gas mark 4, 350° F, 180° C, or until the filling is heated through.

Mix together all the ingredients for the sauce and as soon as the pancakes are hot, pour over some of the sauce and serve the rest in a sauce-boat.

❈ Lockshen Pudding ❈ (d)

There are two versions of this traditional European pudding. This is the creamy one which can be served warm or cold.

12 oz (350 g) flat noodles, cooked
½ oz (15 g) butter
2 oz (50 g) sultanas or raisins
2 eggs
½ pt (¼ l) milk
3 tbsps vanilla sugar*

Mix the cooked, drained noodles with the butter and sultanas and place in a well-greased ovenproof dish. Beat the eggs with the milk and vanilla sugar and pour them over the noodles. Stir well to see that they are covered and bake at gas mark 4, 350° F, 180° C, for about 30 minutes. More milk or sugar may be added to taste.

❈ Caramel Mousse ❈ (d)

This is slightly tricky to make. It uses almost the same ingredients as the famous crème caramel or caramel custard but the result is quite different.

2 eggs, separated
1 tbsp flour

* To make vanilla sugar, split open a vanilla pod and place it in a jar of caster sugar. Leave to infuse for at least one hour. This sugar keeps indefinitely and can be topped up every time you use some for baking.

½ *pt (¼ l) milk*
1 tsp kosher gelatin
1 tbsp water
½ *tsp vanilla essence*

For the caramel
4 oz (125 g) granulated sugar
2½ fl oz (75 ml) water

Whisk the egg yolks with the flour and add a little milk. Heat the rest of the milk and pour it on to the egg yolk mixture. Return to the pan and stir gently to make a custard, being very careful not to let the mixture boil.

Place the sugar in a saucepan, add the water and cook over very low heat until the sugar caramelizes and turns brown. At this moment pour it into the *hot* custard and continue stirring, over low heat, to make sure that there are no solid lumps of caramel and that the mixture is melted and quite smooth. Again, take care not to let the mixture come to the boil.

Mix the gelatin with the water and soften it over heat. Then add this, with the vanilla essence, to the caramel custard mixture. Leave to cool. Whisk the egg whites and gently fold them into the custard.

Grease a mould and spoon in the mousse and chill it well for several hours. Then either turn it out or serve from the mould with some crisp biscuits.

❄ Iced Apricot Mousse ❄ (d) or (p)

1 lb (450 g) fresh apricots (reserve a few for decoration)
¼ *pt (150 ml) water*
6 oz (175 g) caster sugar
1 tsp lemon juice
3 eggs
5 fl oz (150 ml) whipping cream (or parev whip)

Halve and stone the apricots and cook them gently in the water with 3 oz (75 g) sugar until they are soft. (If they are very ripe they will need hardly any cooking.) Purée them with the lemon juice in a blender or by passing them through a sieve, and set aside to cool.

Whisk the eggs with the remaining sugar until they are pale and fluffy and then fold in the cooled apricot purée and the whipped cream or parev whip.

Pour into a dish and freeze for about 3 to 4 hours. Decorate the mousse with a few fresh apricot halves.

❊ Black Cherry Roll ❊ (d)

Do try this intoxicating version of the English trifle.

1 Swiss roll sponge (see Light Sponge Cake, p. 112)
½ lb (225 g) good black cherry jam
3 fl oz (75 ml) whisky or cherry brandy
3 fl oz (75 ml) sherry

For the custard
2 egg yolks
1 tbsp vanilla sugar (see Lockshen Pudding, p. 107)
1 tbsp flour
10 fl oz (¼ l) milk

For decoration
10 fl oz (¼ l) double cream
fresh cherries or grapes

First make the Swiss roll, as in the Light Sponge Cake recipe on p. 112, but using half the mixture for the sponge cake. Bake the mixture in a greased 10-in × 8-in (25-cm × 20-cm) tin for about 10 minutes. When it is cooked, take it out of the oven and turn it on to a sheet of greaseproof paper sprinkled very lightly with flour. Roll it up with the paper and leave to cool. (In this way it won't crack.)

Make the custard with the eggs, sugar, flour and milk (see Custard or *Crème Patissière*, p. 112). Unroll the sponge cake, spread it with the cherry jam and pour over the spirits. Roll it up again, cover with the warm custard and leave it to get quite cold.

After about an hour whip the cream and spread it all over the cake. Decorate with fresh cherries or grapes and chill again before serving.

8. Cakes and Gâteaux

Although many people are concerned about watching their weight, there are many occasions when a cake is appreciated. It doesn't have to be heavy or very rich, and most of the recipes which follow have a light base and are topped with *crème patissière* (custard cream) or fresh berries. European Jews have already adopted the famous cream cakes and pastries of France, Austria and Hungary. Now we are also adding the cheesecakes and 'coffee cakes' of America.

Light Sponge Cake (p)
Custard or *Crème Patissière* (p) or (d)
Glazed Strawberry Flan (p)
Layered Coffee Gâteau (p)
Summer Lemon Cake with Grapes (p) or (d)
Chestnut and Chocolate Gâteau (p)
Crunch-top Almond Flan (p) or (d)
Mille-Feuille with Chinese Gooseberries (d)
Strawberry or Raspberry Cream Gâteau (d)
Sour Cream 'Coffee' Cake (d)
Ginger or Honey Cake (d)
Peach or Cherry Kuchen (d)
Cheesecake: Cooked Cheesecake, Refrigerated Cheesecake (d)
Granny's Apple Cake (d)

❊ Light Sponge Cake ❊   (p)

This cake is the basis for many desserts and gâteaux. Its success
depends on an electric mixer or patience in whisking.

> *5 large eggs*
> *5 oz (150 g) vanilla sugar (see Lockshen Pudding, p. 107)*
> *4½ oz (130 g) self-raising flour*

Preheat the oven to gas mark 7, 425° F, 220° C and warm the
whisk and the bowl you are going to use.

Beat the eggs with the sugar until the mixture is almost white
and very thick. This will take about 5 minutes with an electric
mixer or much longer by hand. Then sift the flour and fold it in,
quickly but very gently, by hand, until it is well mixed with the
eggs and sugar.

Pour the mixture into well-greased tins (this amount makes
enough for 2 8-in (20-cm) round sandwich tins) and cook for
about 12 minutes or until a cocktail stick inserted in the centre
comes out clean and dry. Leave the cakes to cool for a few
minutes before taking them out of the tins and let them get
quite cold before filling or decorating.

❊ Custard or *Crème Patissière* ❊   (p) or (d)

This is a custard which can be used in numerous cakes and is
the basis for many desserts. It is worth making as it is quick and
can be adapted to both milk and parev recipes.

> Parev version
> *½ pt (¼ l) water*
> *6 tbsps parev 'milk' powder*
> *2 eggs*
> *3 tbsps vanilla sugar (see Lockshen Pudding, p. 107)*
> *2 tbsps plain flour*

Milk version
½ pt (¼ l) creamy milk
2 eggs
3 tbsps vanilla sugar
2 tbsps plain flour

For the parev version, boil the water and add the parev 'milk' powder, stirring until there are no lumps. Then treat exactly like milk.

Heat the milk until it boils. Whisk the eggs with the vanilla sugar and add the flour. Pour a little boiling milk on to the egg mixture and then pour all this back into the saucepan with the rest of the milk. Continue stirring, over low heat, until the custard thickens. Leave it to cool and then use it as a cream filling on its own or mixed with whipped cream or parev whip to taste.

❋ Glazed Strawberry Flan ❋   (p)

For the pastry
8 oz (200 g) plain flour
5 oz (125 g) butter or margarine
4 tbsps water
1 egg yolk
1 tbsp icing sugar

For the filling
½ pt (¼ l) Crème Patissière (see p. 112)
1 lb (450 g) fresh strawberries
3 tbsps redcurrant jelly, melted and cooled
1 egg white

First make the pastry (for method, see pp. 52–3), adding the icing sugar with the flour. Roll the dough out to fill an 8-in (20-cm) flan tin and bake blind at gas mark 7, 425° F, 220° C for about 20 minutes or until it is crisp and golden. Leave the pastry case to get quite cold.

Meanwhile make the *crème patissière*. Brush the base of the flan case with a little egg white (this helps to prevent it getting soggy from the custard) and then fill it with the cold *crème patissière*. Arrange the halved strawberries all over the top and brush them over with melted redcurrant jelly. Serve the flan soon after it is made.

Note : in winter, halved white and black grapes make a good alternative to strawberries.

❖ Layered Coffee Gâteau ❖ (p)

This is a rich dessert which keeps well. It is a good idea, if you can, to freeze the sponge cake rounds before you assemble the gâteau. If they are firm you can cut them horizontally into thin layers before adding the filling.

For the cake
2 × 8-in (20-cm) sponge rounds (see Light Sponge Cake, p. 112)

For the rum syrup
¼ pt (150 ml) strong coffee
2 tbsps granulated sugar
2 tbsps rum

For the coffee filling
7½ fl oz (225 ml) strong coffee
6 oz (175 g) caster sugar
4 egg yolks
6 tbsps parev 'milk' powder
12 oz (350 g) margarine

For decoration
4 oz (125 g) toasted almonds

Bake the sponge cakes, leave them to cool, and cut them across to make four layers.

Boil the coffee and sugar together for about 3 minutes, add the rum and leave the syrup to cool.

For the filling, again boil the coffee and sugar and after a few minutes pour this syrup on to the egg yolks, beating all the time until the mixture is very soft. While it is still hot add the parev 'milk' powder and then whisk in the margarine, piece by piece, until the mixture is very thick. Chill well.

Brush the first layer of cake with the rum syrup, cover with some of the coffee filling, place another layer on top and continue like this with the other three layers.

Spread the coffee filling carefully over the top and decorate the cake with toasted almonds. Chill well before serving.

Summer Lemon Cake with Grapes (p) or (d)

For the cake
4 eggs
4 oz (125 g) caster sugar
3¾ oz (100 g) self-raising flour
grated rind of 1 lemon

For the filling
1 egg
4 oz (125 g) caster sugar
grated rind and juice of 1 lemon
1 oz (25 g) plain flour
¼ pt (150 ml) whipped cream or parev whip

For decoration
grapes or pineapple

First make the sponge cake (see Light Sponge Cake, p. 112) using grated lemon rind instead of vanilla flavouring. Bake in a 10-in (25-cm) single layer sponge tin and leave to cool while you make the filling.

Beat together the egg and sugar and add the grated lemon rind and juice. Fold in the flour and cook the mixture over low heat until it thickens. Allow to cool and then fold in the whipped cream or parev whip and pile the mixture on to the sponge cake.

Decorate with halved grapes or pineapple and chill well before serving.

❊ Chestnut and Chocolate Gâteau ❊　　　　　　(p)

> 1 12-in (30-cm) sponge cake (see Light Sponge Cake,
>   p. 112)
> 8 oz (225 g) chestnut purée, unsweetened
> 3 oz (75 g) icing sugar
> 1 tsp vanilla essence (or use vanilla sugar)
> 2 oz (50 g) plain chocolate
> 2 tbsps rum or chocolate liqueur

First make the sponge base and leave it to cool. Beat the chestnut purée with the vanilla and sugar until it is quite smooth and there are no lumps. Brush the cake with the rum or liqueur and then either pipe the chestnut mixture over the top or rub it through a sieve.

Melt the chocolate over a pan of simmering water and when it is soft drizzle it with a small pointed spoon all over the chestnut.

Note : this cake is also very good served with vanilla ice cream or fresh cream.

❊ Crunch-top Almond Flan ❊　　　　　　(p) or (d)

> 6 oz (175 g) flan pastry (for method, see p. 113)
> 4 oz (125 g) ground almonds
> 4 oz (125 g) caster sugar
> 1 egg, separated
> 2 oz (50 g) margarine or butter (reserve 1 tbsp)
> 2 oz (50 g) granulated sugar (reserve 1 tbsp)
> 2 oz (50 g) self-raising flour
> 2 oz (50 g) almonds, flaked

Line an 8-in (20-cm) flan tin with the pastry and bake blind for 10 minutes at gas mark 7, 425° F, 220° C.

Mix the ground almonds with the caster sugar and make it into a paste with the egg white. Spread this over the pastry base.

Mix the margarine or butter with the sugar, stir in the egg

yolk and add the flour. Spoon this mixture over the almond paste and bake for a further 10 minutes at gas mark 4, 350° F, 180° C. Take it out of the oven, scatter over the flaked almonds and sprinkle it with 1 tablespoon of sugar. Drizzle over 1 table-spoon melted margarine or butter and return to the oven for about 10 minutes, when the top will be slightly brown and crunchy and the cake just cooked.

❊ *Mille-Feuille* with **Chinese Gooseberries** ❊   (d)

The brilliant green of sliced chinese gooseberries (kiwi fruit) gives this pastry a very unusual and attractive appearance. Of course, other fruit like strawberries, peaches or apricots may be used instead.

> *4 oz (125 g) puff pastry*
> *¼ pt (150 ml) double cream*
> *2 tsps caster sugar*
> *2 tsps apricot jam*
> *2 chinese gooseberries (or other fruit)*

Roll the pastry out into two thin rectangles. Mark one into slices and bake them on an ungreased tin in a hot oven (gas mark 7, 425° F, 220° C), for about 15 minutes or until they are puffed and golden. (They will shrink a little in size in the oven.)

Leave the pastry to cool, and then assemble the gâteau just before you are ready to serve it. Whisk the cream until it is very thick and then fold in the sugar. Brush the unmarked rectangle of pastry with apricot jam, and cover it with a layer of whipped cream and some sliced chinese gooseberries. Put the other layer of pastry on top, spread with the rest of the cream and arrange the remaining sliced fruit down the centre.

❊ **Strawberry or Raspberry Cream Gâteau** ❊   (d)

> For the cake
> *6 eggs*

6 oz (170 g) vanilla sugar (see Lockshen Pudding, p. 107)
5½ oz (155 g) self-raising flour

For the filling and topping
1 lb (450 g) fresh strawberries or raspberries
½–¾ pt (300–425 ml) double cream
1 tbsp icing sugar

First make the sponge cake (see Light Sponge Cake, p. 112) in a 10-in (25-cm) tin and leave it to cool. Split it in half and put one half on a flat plate or serving dish. Whisk the cream until it is thick and then spread most of it on to the base of the cake. Cover with the sliced strawberries or raspberries (reserving a few for decoration). Carefully put the other sponge cake on top and sift the icing sugar over it. Decorate with a few strawberries and pipe a little cream around the outside.

Note: if you like a slightly sweeter taste, add some sugar to the whipped cream or fruit.

❅ Sour Cream 'Coffee' Cake ❅ (d)

This cake has a deceptively 'ordinary' appearance but a lovely flavour.

For 2 small cakes
7 oz (200 g) butter
4 oz (115 g) caster sugar
3 large eggs
12 fl oz (375 ml) sour cream or natural yogurt
10 oz (275 g) self-raising flour
1 tsp bicarbonate of soda
1 tsp baking powder

For the topping
1 oz (25 g) granulated sugar
1 oz (25 g) demerara sugar
1 oz (25 g) chopped nuts
½ tsp cinnamon

Soften the butter and cream it with the sugar. Add the beaten eggs and the sour cream and then fold in the sifted dry ingredients. Mix together the sugar, nuts and cinnamon and sprinkle the topping over the cake. Bake in 2 round 8-in (20-cm) cake tins (about 1 in (2½ cm) deep) at gas mark 4, 350° F, 180° C for about 30 minutes.

❊ Ginger or Honey Cake ❊ (d)

This type of cake is a Jewish speciality served at New Year. The ingredients vary but the dark, moist characteristic of the cake depends on using either honey or golden syrup.

> *4 oz (110 g) demerara sugar*
> *3 oz (75 g) butter*
> *6 oz (175 g) golden syrup or honey*
> *¼ pt (150 ml) milk*
> *8 oz (225 g) self-raising flour*
> *¼ tsp salt*
> *¾ tsp ground ginger*
> *1 tsp baking powder*
> *¼ tsp bicarbonate of soda*
> *1 egg*

Grease and line a 1-lb (450-g) loaf tin and preheat the oven to gas mark 3, 325° F, 160° C.

Warm the sugar, butter and syrup in a pan over low heat until the sugar has melted, but do not let it boil. Warm the milk and add it with the sugar mixture to the sifted dry ingredients. Add the beaten egg and stir well. Pour the mixture into the cake tin and bake for about 1 hour. Leave to cool.

This cake is at its best a few days after baking, so wrap it in foil and try not to eat it immediately.

❀ **Peach or Cherry Kuchen** ❀   (d)

12 oz (350 g) self-raising flour
8 oz (225 g) caster sugar
6 oz (175 g) butter
2 eggs
8 tbsps milk
6 large peaches or 1 lb (450 g) fresh or frozen cherries
4 oz (125 g) soft brown sugar
½ tsp cinnamon

Grease and line an 8-in × 10-in (20-cm × 25-cm), 1-in (2½-cm)
deep cake tin and preheat the oven to gas mark 5, 375° F, 190° C.

Mix together the flour, sugar, softened butter, eggs and milk
until you have a smooth batter. Pour this into the cake tin and
arrange the fruit over it. If you are using peaches, peel and slice
them—with cherries, remove the stones. Sprinkle the top with
a mixture of brown sugar and cinnamon and bake for about
40 minutes.

This cake can be served straight from the oven, or cut into
squares when cold.

❀ **Cheesecake** ❀   (d)

There are many different variations of this recipe. The first
one has no base and needs gentle cooking. The refrigerated
version has a lemon flavour and a mousse-like texture.

COOKED CHEESECAKE

5 eggs, separated
5 oz (150 g) caster sugar
1 lb (450 g) curd cheese
6 fl oz (175 ml) sour cream
1 tsp vanilla essence
2 tbsps self-raising flour

Beat the egg yolks with the sugar and when they are pale and thick, add the curd cheese. Mix in the sour cream and vanilla and then fold in the stiffly whipped egg whites with the flour. Pour into a greased 8-in (20-cm) cake tin and bake at gas mark 1, 275° F, 140° C for 70 minutes. Turn the oven off and leave for a further hour *without opening the door*. Then take the cake out and leave to cool before removing from the tin.

REFRIGERATED CHEESECAKE

8 oz (225 g) biscuit crumbs, crushed
3 oz (75 g) butter, melted
12 oz (350 g) curd cheese (or cream cheese)
3 eggs, separated
3 oz (75 g) caster sugar
1½–2 tbsps kosher gelatin
2½ fl oz (75 ml) lemon juice
¼ pt (150 ml) double cream

Mix the crushed biscuit crumbs with the melted butter and press round the sides and base of a loose-bottomed 8-in (20-cm) cake tin. Bake at gas mark 6, 400° F, 200° C for 10 minutes.

Mix the cream cheese with the egg yolks and 2 oz (50 g) sugar and beat till smooth. Soften the gelatin and lemon juice (see Melon with Fresh Orange Jelly, p. 32) and when it has cooled add it to the cream cheese mixture. Whisk the egg whites and fold them in, with the rest of the sugar and the whipped cream, to the cheese mixture. Pour into the cooled biscuit crust and chill the cake for a few hours.

Both these cakes can be served with strawberries, cherries or blackcurrants.

❊ Granny's Apple Cake ❊ (d)

For the cake
6 oz (175 g) self-raising flour
1 tsp baking powder

3 oz (75 g) caster sugar
1 large egg
6 tbsps milk
1 oz (25 g) butter, melted
3 cooking apples

For the topping
1 oz (25 g) butter, melted
2 oz (50 g) caster sugar
½ tsp cinnamon

Grease and line an 8-in (20-cm) square cake tin and preheat the oven to gas mark 6, 400° F, 200° C.

Mix the flour with the baking powder and sugar. Whisk the egg with the milk and melted butter and pour this mixture into the flour, stirring well. Pour into the cake tin. Peel, core and slice the apples and cover the cake with them.

For the topping, brush the apples with the rest of the melted butter and sprinkle over the sugar and cinnamon.

Bake in a hot oven for about 35 minutes. After 25 minutes cover with a sheet of foil if the cake is getting too brown and test to see if the cake is done by inserting a cocktail stick in the centre. If it comes out dry the cake is cooked.

9. *Biscuits and Small Pastries*

The use of almonds, dates and figs goes back to Biblical times, and spices like cinnamon and ginger feature in nearly all Jewish sweetmeats. For some people 'traditional' means thin phyllo pastry flavoured with orange-flower water; for others it means crumbly pastry with dried fruit. However, all the biscuits and pastries in this chapter have one thing in common—you can make them at your leisure and freeze them. In this way you will always have something good to bring out for an unexpected guest.

Sweet Chestnut Tartlets (p)
Queijinhos (p)
Stuffed Dates (p)
Strudel Slices (p)
Rolled Phyllo Pastries (p)
Éclairs (p)
Butter Biscuits (d)
Thin Biscuits (Crackers) (d)
Chocolate Dipped Biscuits (d)
Butter Pastries (d) or (p)
Cinnamon Buns (d)
Dutch Butter Cake (d)
Orange Rolls (d)
Hamantaschen (d)

Sweet Chestnut Tartlets (p)

6 oz (175 g) flan pastry (see basic rich pastry, p. 52)
8 oz (225 g) chestnut purée, unsweetened

4 tbsps icing sugar
1 tsp vanilla essence

For decoration
pistachio nuts or toasted almonds

Make the pastry and cut out small boat or tartlet cases. Bake at gas mark 7, 425° F, 220° C for about 12 minutes until they are crisp, and leave to cool.

Mix the chestnut purée with the sugar and vanilla essence and pipe or pile the mixture into the tartlet cases. Decorate with halved pistachios or almonds.

This amount of chestnut filling makes about 16 tartlets.

❈ Queijinhos ❈ (p)

The word means 'little cheeses' because of the shape of these traditional sweets. They are based on a Portuguese speciality called 'jemma'—a sweet golden filling which just has to be tasted, so don't be put off by the lengthy instructions.

For the cases
2 oz (50 g) caster sugar
3 fl oz (90 ml) water
5 oz (150 g) ground almonds

For the jemma filling
4 oz (125 g) caster sugar
2½ fl oz (75 ml) water
1 vanilla pod
6 egg yolks

Make a syrup with the 2 oz (50 g) sugar and 3 fl oz (90 ml) water. Bring to the boil and keep on the heat for about 2 minutes. Add it to the ground almonds to make a paste.

To prepare the filling, put the sugar, water and vanilla pod in a small pan. Bring it to the boil, stirring once or twice until the sugar has melted. Once the syrup starts to boil do not stir

it, but wash down the sides of the pan with a wet pastry brush.
Continue boiling and brushing until the syrup makes a thread
when tested between the thumb and first finger. At this stage
pour it slowly on to the beaten egg yolks. Return the mixture
to a double saucepan and stir until it thickens—but do not let
it boil. Then immediately stand the pan in cold water.

Roll the almond paste into small balls, the size of a walnut,
and make flat discs for the lids. Form each ball into a cup and
fill each one with the cold jemma mixture. Seal with a lid and
continue until all the almond paste is used up (this quantity
makes about 20). The finished sweets should be about $\frac{3}{4}$ in (2 cm)
high and may be rolled in granulated sugar and stored in the
refrigerator or freezer.

❖ Stuffed Dates ❖   (p)

These are traditional Sephardi sweets eaten at Purim.

5 oz (150 g) ground almonds
2 oz (50 g) caster sugar
3 fl oz (90 ml) water
1 box preserved dates

For the caramel
4 oz (125 g) granulated sugar
6 fl oz (180 ml) water
1 dsp liquid glucose

First make the almond paste with the ground almonds, sugar
and water (see previous recipe). Stone each date and fill with a
small, rolled piece of almond paste.

To make the caramel, bring the sugar, water and glucose to
the boil, stirring once or twice. Then stop stirring and continue
boiling until the syrup reaches the crack stage (about 280° F,
140° C). You can test this by drizzling a little syrup into cold
water—if it forms needles which snap, the syrup is ready.
Take it off the heat, drop the dates in one by one, remove and
place them on an oiled surface. Leave until quite cold when

they will come away easily. Wipe the bases to remove any oil and place in sweet cases.

❈ Strudel Slices ❈   (p)

For the pastry
5 oz (150 g) margarine
4 oz (125 g) plain flour
4 oz (125 g) self-raising flour
1 oz (25 g) ground almonds
2 oz (50 g) caster sugar
1 egg, separated

For the filling
6 oz (175 g) mixed dried fruit, soaked for 10 minutes in
  boiling water and then drained
1 oz (25 g) caster sugar
1 tsp cinnamon

Rub the margarine into the flours until the mixture is like fine crumbs. Add the ground almonds and 1 oz (25 g) of the sugar. Then add the egg yolk and mix to a dough. Chill this in the refrigerator while you make the filling.

Soak and drain the dried fruit and mix it with the sugar and cinnamon.

Roll the dough out into 3 or 4 rectangles and spread the filling down the centre of each one. Fold the side edges over to enclose the filling and place them, with the seam underneath, on a lightly greased baking sheet. Brush the rolls with slightly beaten egg white and sprinkle with the remaining sugar. Mark into slices about 1 in (2½ cm) thick and bake at gas mark 4, 350° F, 180° C for about 25 to 30 minutes, or until the strudel is a light golden colour. Remove from the tin carefully and cool. When cold, cut into slices and store in an airtight tin or the freezer.

❋ Rolled Phyllo Pastries ❋ (p)

The paper-thin pastry needed for these Middle Eastern biscuits
is available from Greek delicatessens. Apart from that all you
need is time and patience!

¾ lb (350 g) almonds
6 oz (175 g) caster sugar
1 tsp cardamom
2 tsps rose water
1 lb (450 g) phyllo pastry
2 tbsps oil

Chop the almonds very finely but do not grind them. Mix them
with the sugar, spice and rose water. Using a little of the pastry
at a time (it goes dry if left open to the air for too long), cut it
into 4-in (10-cm) squares. Spread a spoonful of the almond
mixture on each square, place another square on top and fold
over ½ in (1½ cm) of two opposite corners. Then take a pencil and
roll the unfolded ends round it. Gently remove the pencil, leaving a hollow inside. Place the rolls on a greased baking sheet,
brush lightly with oil and bake at gas mark 2, 300° F, 150° C
for about 20 minutes.

This amount makes a very large quantity of crisp, golden
biscuits but they store very well and can be eaten almost straight
from the freezer.

❋ Éclairs ❋ (p)

This is a non-cream version of a very famous pastry. Imitation
cream on its own is no substitute for the real filling, but made
this way it is very good indeed.

For the choux paste
2 oz (50 g) margarine
¼ pt (150 ml) water
4 oz (125 g) plain flour

pinch salt
drop vanilla essence
3 eggs

For the filling
½ pt (¼ l) Crème Patissière (see p. 112)
1 oz (25 g) melted chocolate
2 fl oz (50 ml) parev whip

For the topping
1 tsp cocoa or *1 tsp instant coffee*
8 oz (225 g) icing sugar or *chocolate sauce (see Pear and Walnut Tart with Chocolate Sauce, p. 100)*
1 tbsp warm water

To make the choux paste, melt the margarine in the water and bring to the boil. Add all the flour and stir quickly until the mixture comes away from the sides of the pan into a ball. Cool this 'panada' slightly and then add the salt, vanilla and beaten eggs, one at a time, beating vigorously between each one. The mixture should be very smooth and shiny. Put it into a forcing bag and with a knife dipped in water, pipe it out and cut into 3-in (7½-cm) lengths on a greased tin. Cook in a preheated oven at gas mark 7, 425° F, 220° C for about 30 minutes until the éclairs are golden and puffed. Take out any soft inside and leave to cool.

For the filling, mix the *crème patissière* with the melted chocolate and parev whip and fill each éclair with the mixture.

Mix the cocoa and water and stir in enough icing sugar to make the icing, then spread it over the éclairs.

Variation: use coffee icing instead and add some coffee flavouring to the filling. For *profiteroles*, make small buns out of the choux paste, fill them and pile them up in a pyramid. Cover them with hot chocolate sauce and serve immediately.

❈ **Butter Biscuits** ❈   (d) or (p)

In spite of their name, these biscuits are almost as good made
with margarine. They can be stored in a tin or the freezer (and
can, in fact, be eaten frozen).

> *5 oz (150 g) butter or margarine*
> *8 oz (225 g) self-raising flour*
> *5 oz (150 g) caster sugar (reserve 1 tbsp)*
> *½ tsp cinnamon*
> *1 egg, separated*
> *2 tbsps cold water*
> *2 oz (50 g) almonds, flaked*

Preheat the oven to gas mark 4, 350° F, 180° C.

Rub the butter into the flour and add the sugar and cinnamon.
Mix to a firm paste with the egg yolk and cold water and roll it
out about ¼ in (½ cm) thick. Cut the biscuits into rounds and
place them on an ungreased baking sheet. Press a few flaked
almonds on to each biscuit and then brush them with slightly
beaten egg white. Sprinkle with 1 tablespoon of sugar and bake
for about 15 minutes, when they will be a golden colour. They
will be soft when they come out of the oven, but remove them
immediately from the baking sheet and leave to cool on a wire
tray. When cold they will harden.

This amount makes about 50 flaky biscuits.

❈ **Thin Biscuits (Crackers)** ❈   (d)

These are served buttered, with cheese—they are unlike any
bought crispbread and need very few ingredients. Do roll them
out really thin—this is what makes them good.

> *8 oz (225 g) plain flour*
> *pinch salt*
> *1 tsp baking powder*
> *1 oz (25 g) butter, melted*
> *3 fl oz (75 ml) milk, warmed*

Sieve the flour, salt and baking powder into a basin. Make a well in the centre and pour in the melted butter and warmed milk. Mix it all together and knead until the dough is free from cracks. Then on a lightly floured board, roll it out until it is almost paper-thin. Cut into squares, prick with a fork and bake on greased tins at gas mark 5, 375° F, 190° C for about 10 minutes. The biscuits will be pale gold and very brittle.

✻ Chocolate Dipped Biscuits ✻   (d)

These ingredients will make a large quantity of biscuits. Taken straight from the freezer they are crisp and very attractive. Make only half the quantity if you don't plan to keep some.

   1 lb (450 g) butter
   ½ lb (225 g) caster sugar
   1½ lb (675 g) plain flour
   ¼ lb (125 g) cooking chocolate

Soften the butter and cream it with the sugar. Add the flour and mix to a biscuit dough. Then either roll it and cut into shapes or use a forcing gadget to make piped biscuits. Bake at gas mark 7, 425° F, 220° C, for about 10 minutes. Place them on a wire tray while you melt the chocolate in a bowl over hot water. Take the cooled biscuits and dip one half of each into the melted chocolate, then place them back on the wire tray to cool.

✻ Butter Pastries ✻   (d) or (p)

The recipe sounds complicated but is in fact easy. They look like round Danish pastries and are good either straight from the oven or cooled and with a little icing drizzled over.

   5 oz (140 g) soft butter
   8 oz (225 g) self-raising flour
   ¼ pt (150 ml) milk

2 oz (50 g) sultanas
2 oz (50 g) granulated sugar
2 oz (50 g) icing sugar for optional icing

Make a dough by mixing 2 oz (50 g) butter with the flour and adding the milk. Roll it out on a floured board and spread half the remaining butter over the top two-thirds of the rectangle of pastry. Sprinkle this with 1 oz (25 g) sultanas and 1 oz (25 g) sugar and fold the unbuttered portion up and the top portion over. Turn the folded dough round and roll it in the other direction to form a rectangle. Spread the remaining butter all over this and sprinkle over the rest of the sultanas and sugar. Now roll the dough over like a Swiss roll and cut it into 1-in (2½-cm) thick slices. Arrange these on a greased baking sheet and cook at gas mark 4, 350° F, 180° C for about 30 minutes. They will rise and spread slightly.

The buttery flavour is best when they are eaten hot. If they are left to cool, drizzle a little white icing over the tops for decoration.

This amount makes about 16 butter pastries.

❋ Cinnamon Buns ❋   (d)

For the buns
2 oz (50 g) butter
2 oz (50 g) caster sugar
2 eggs
2 oz (50 g) plain flour
½ tsp baking powder

For the syrup
2½ fl oz (75 ml) water
2 oz (50 g) caster sugar

For sprinkling
1 oz (25 g) granulated sugar
½ tsp cinnamon

Cream the butter with the sugar, add the beaten eggs and fold in the sifted flour and baking powder. Spoon the mixture into greased bun tins and bake at gas mark 5, 375° F, 190° C for about 20 minutes or until they are cooked.

Meanwhile boil the water and sugar together and when the buns are cooked pass them immediately through the syrup and then roll them in the mixed sugar and cinnamon. Leave to cool.

This amount makes about 10 cinnamon buns.

❈ Dutch Butter Cake ❈   (d)

4 oz (125 g) self-raising flour
4 oz (125 g) plain flour
3 oz (75 g) caster sugar
½ tsp cinnamon
6 oz (175 g) butter
1 egg, separated
1 heaped tsp jelly marmalade
2 oz (50 g) almonds or walnuts

Mix the flours, sugar and cinnamon together and then rub in the butter until the mixture is crumbly. Add the yolk of the egg and the marmalade and then press the mixture into an 8-in × 10-in (20-cm × 25-cm) greased cake tin. Lightly whisk the egg white with a fork and brush over the top. Mark into squares will be golden-brown and quite soft in the centre, but Bake at gas mark 5, 375° F, 190° C for about 25 minutes. The squares will be golden-brown and quite soft in the centre, but they harden slightly as they cool.

❈ Orange Rolls ❈   (d)

For the cake
3 large eggs
3 oz (75 g) caster sugar

$2\frac{1}{2}$ oz (60 g) self-raising flour
grated rind of 1 orange

For the filling
$\frac{1}{2}$ pt ($\frac{1}{4}$ l) double cream
juice of 1 orange
1 tbsp caster sugar

Preheat the oven to gas mark 7, 425° F, 220° C. Make a Swiss roll sponge mixture (see Light Sponge Cake, p. 112), using the grated orange rind as flavouring. Line a large, shallow 12-in × 10-in (30-cm × 25-cm) baking tin with greaseproof paper and bake the sponge for about 10 minutes. When it is cooked turn it on to very lightly floured greaseproof paper, cut into 3-in × 5-in ($7\frac{1}{2}$-cm × $12\frac{1}{2}$-cm) rectangles and roll each one up into miniature Swiss rolls.

Whisk the cream until it is very thick. Fold in the orange juice and freeze the mixture for about 10 minutes. Unwrap the cooled sponges, pipe the orange cream down the centre and roll up again. Chill well and serve spinkled with a little extra sugar.

This amount makes about 8 orange rolls.

❊ Hamantaschen ❊   (d)

This is a quick version of the Purim speciality. It is made with a cakey dough and not the traditional yeast dough—also the filling is not too sweet as it is made with prunes rather than the German 'mohn' or poppy seeds.

For the dough
4 oz (115 g) butter
4 oz (115 g) caster sugar
1 egg
8 oz (230 g) plain flour
1 tsp baking powder
2 tbsps milk
1 tsp vanilla essence

For the filling
6 oz (170 g) prunes
1 tsp lemon juice

Cream the butter and the sugar. Add the egg and then the sifted flour and baking powder. Mix to a soft dough with the milk and vanilla essence and leave to chill in the refrigerator while you make the filling.

Pour boiling water over the prunes and then drain them and remove the stones. Chop the prunes finely.

Roll the dough out about $\frac{1}{4}$ in ($\frac{1}{2}$ cm) thick and cut it into 3-in ($7\frac{1}{2}$-cm) rounds. Put a small spoonful of the filling on each round and then lift up the edges to form a three-cornered pastry, pinching the sides together. Place on a lightly greased baking sheet and bake at gas mark 5, 375° F, 190° C for about 20 minutes.

10. Breads

Yeast breads are a pleasure to make. They do take time but are much easier than people believe. When you have mastered the main principles, it is a good idea to make the dough in large quantities. You can then make up a selection of sweet loaves and buns and freeze them. It takes only a little time to re-heat them and serve them warm with coffee.

In the recipes I use strong flour, which is a white flour with a high gluten content especially good for bread and yeast baking. Also, I like to use fresh yeast which is easily obtainable from health food shops. However, if you prefer to use dried, you just need to halve the quantity of yeast given in the recipes.

YEAST BREADS
Challa (p)
Pita (p)
Caraway 'Rye' Rolls (p)
Bagels (p)
Cinnamon Loaf or Whirls (d)
Nut Bread (d)
Apricot Danish Ring (d)
Iced Almond Fingers (d)

QUICK BREADS
Walnut Loaf (d)
Orange Loaf or Buns (d)
Date Bread (d)

✳ Challa ✳   (p)

This is the plaited white loaf, traditionally made with eggs and
sprinkled with poppy seeds. Two loaves are always on the table
for the Friday night meal and one for the Sabbath meal.

> ½ oz (15 g) fresh yeast
> 8 fl oz (225 ml) warm water
> 1 tbsp caster sugar
> 1 oz (25 g) margarine, melted
> 1½ tsps salt
> 1 egg
> 1 lb (450 g) strong white flour
>
> For the glaze
> 1 egg, beaten
> poppy seeds

Mix the yeast with half the warm water and sugar and leave
until it starts to froth slightly. Then add the margarine, salt and
beaten egg and some of the flour. Continue adding flour and the
rest of the liquid until a dough is formed.

Knead the dough for a few minutes and then leave it to prove
(rise) until it has doubled in size (about 1 hour). Knock back
the dough and then form it into plaited loaves. To do this
divide the mixture into 2, then each of these into 3 pieces.
Roll each one into a long sausage shape and plait 3 together
to make each loaf. Leave the loaves on a greased tin to prove
again (about 15 minutes). Brush gently with the beaten egg,
sprinkle with the poppy seeds and bake in a preheated oven
(gas mark 7, 425° F, 220° C) for about 35 minutes, or until the
loaves are a deep golden-brown. Leave to cool on a wire tray.

✳ Pita ✳   (p)

This is the Middle Eastern flat bread, which, when baked, has a hollow inside. In Israel it is filled with spicy falafel balls and salad, but is equally good served with kebabs. Do reheat it before eating as it is one of the few breads that are really not good cold.

$\frac{1}{2}$ *oz (15 g) fresh yeast*
pinch caster sugar
$\frac{1}{4}$ *pt (125 ml) cold water*
$\frac{1}{4}$ *pt (125 ml) boiling water*
2 tbsps oil
1 lb (450 g) strong white flour
$\frac{1}{2}$ *tsp salt*

Put the yeast in a bowl and sprinkle on the sugar. Pour the waters into a jug and mix the yeast with $\frac{1}{4}$ of the liquid. Leave in a warm place until the yeast starts to froth, then add the oil, the rest of the water and the flour sifted with the salt. Knead well for about 10 minutes and then leave the dough to prove (about 1 hour). Roll the pita into ovals and place them on a floured cloth. Heat the oven to gas mark 9, 500° F, 260° C, and put in the greased baking trays. After about 15 minutes when the pita will have risen again, press them down and place them on the very hot baking sheets and bake for about 10 minutes.

❀ Caraway 'Rye' Rolls ❀ (p)

Rye bread is a Jewish favourite, and I believe what some people like is not so much the firm close texture of a rye loaf but the taste of the caraway seeds, so I have adapted this with whole-meal rolls, which are easy to make when rye flour is not available.

$\frac{1}{2}$ *oz (15 g) fresh yeast*
8 fl oz (225 ml) warm water
1 oz (25 g) oil or margarine
1 tsp salt
1 tbsp caster sugar
1 egg
$\frac{1}{2}$ *lb (225 g) strong white flour*

$\frac{1}{2}$ *lb (225 g) granary or wholemeal flour*
1 tbsp caraway seeds

Make the bread dough in the same way as the Challa (see p. 136), using a mixture of the two flours. (This makes a lighter bread than using all wholemeal.) Finally add the seeds and leave to prove for about an hour. Then knock back the dough, divide it into small rolls and place them on a greased tin to prove again for about 15 minutes. Sprinkle them with a little flour and bake in a preheated oven (gas mark 7, 425° F, 220° C), for about 10 to 15 minutes.

❄ Bagels ❄ (p)

According to legend bagels were originally stirrup-shaped rolls created by a baker in Poland to commemorate a battle victory by his king. The hard, crusty rings known as beigels were well known all over Europe, and the large American bagel with its different toppings of onion, sesame or poppy seeds, is now a favourite breakfast roll, often served with cream cheese and smoked salmon.

The unusual boiling process alters the density of the dough and removes much of the starch, so what seems like a slightly heavy bread is in fact more digestible and less fattening than one would think.

1 oz (25 g) fresh yeast
2 tbsps caster sugar
8 fl oz (200 ml) lukewarm water
15 oz (425 g) strong flour
1 tsp salt

For optional topping
$\frac{1}{2}$ *onion, finely chopped*, or *1 tbsp poppy or sesame seeds*

Mix the yeast with 1 tablespoon of sugar and a little water. Sift the flour with the salt and when the yeast mixture starts to froth (after about 10 minutes) mix it with the flour and the rest of the water to form a firm dough. Knead well for about 10 minutes and then cut into 12 pieces. Knead each piece and roll it into a rope about 7 in (18 cm) long. Wind it round your hand and roll it well to seal the joint. Place the bagels on a well-floured board and leave them to prove for about an hour.

Turn the oven to gas mark 10, 500° F, 250° C and have ready a large pan of boiling water. When the rolls have risen slightly (but not as much as normal rolls) place them, one at a time, in the boiling water and as soon as they rise to the top turn them over. Boil for 2 minutes and then drain them and lay them on a greased tray. Put them in the oven and after one minute turn them over* and continue baking for about 15 minutes or until they are brown and shiny. This amount makes 12 large bagels.

❖ Cinnamon Loaf or Whirls ❖ (d)

For the dough
$\frac{1}{2}$ oz (15 g) fresh yeast
8 fl oz (225 ml) warm milk or water
1 oz (25 g) butter
2 tbsps caster sugar
$\frac{1}{2}$ tsp salt
1 egg
1 lb (450 g) strong white flour

For the filling
6 tbsps soft brown sugar
$1\frac{1}{2}$ tsps cinnamon
3 tsps sultanas

For decoration
white icing

Make the dough as for the Challa (see p. 136). Leave it to prove and then knead it well.

To make the cinnamon loaves, divide the dough into two and roll each one into a rectangle. Mix the brown sugar, cinnamon

* Sprinkle them with chopped onion or seeds before the final baking if you like a flavouring, otherwise leave them plain.

and sultanas and sprinkle them over the rolled-out dough. Roll each long side towards the centre and then turn the loaf over with the seam underneath and place in a greased 1-lb (450-g) loaf tin. Prove again for 15 minutes, cover with foil and bake at gas mark 6, 400° F, 200° C, for about 10 minutes. Then turn the oven down slightly and continue cooking for a further 30 minutes. Remove from the tin and cool. When cold serve sliced and buttered.

This amount makes 2 loaves.

To make whirls, roll out the rectangles, spread with the cinnamon, sugar and sultana mixture and roll up as for a Swiss roll. Cut into 1-in (2½-cm) slices and place these on a greased baking sheet in a circle, just touching each other. Leave to prove again and bake as above for about 25 minutes. Drizzle with white icing and serve either hot or cold.

❖ Nut Bread ❖ (d)

For the dough
½ oz (15 g) fresh yeast
2 oz (50 g) caster sugar
5 fl oz (150 ml) milk, warmed
4 oz (125 g) butter
1 egg
1 egg yolk
14 oz (400 g) strong white flour

For the filling
3½ oz (100 g) nuts, chopped
2 oz (50 g) cake or biscuit crumbs
2 oz (50 g) soft brown sugar
1 small egg
1 tbsp water

To make the dough, mix the yeast with 1 oz (25 g) sugar, add half the warm milk and leave to froth for a few minutes. Melt the butter in the rest of the milk and then add this, with the remaining sugar, egg, and egg yolk, to the flour. Knead for a few minutes and leave to prove for about 1 hour.

Meanwhile prepare the filling. Mix the nuts with the crumbs and brown sugar and moisten with the beaten egg and water.

When the dough has risen to about double its size, knead it again and then cut it into 2 pieces (this quantity makes 2 7-in × 4-in (17½-cm × 10-cm) loaves). Roll each one into a rectangle and spread with the filling. Roll each side towards the centre and place the loaf, seam side up, into a greased 1-lb (450-g) loaf tin. Cook in a preheated oven (gas mark 6, 400° F, 200° C), for about 10 minutes, then turn the oven to gas mark 5, 375° F, 190° C and continue cooking, covering the loaf with foil if it starts to brown, for about 40 minutes. Remove from the tin and cool.

Serve the bread sliced with fresh unsalted butter.

❊ Apricot Danish Ring ❊   (d)

½ *quantity sweet dough as in previous recipe*
4 oz (125 g) dried apricots, soaked in boiling water for 40 minutes
1 oz (25 g) caster sugar
½ *oz (15 g) butter, melted*
1 oz (25 g) almonds, flaked

For decoration
white icing

Make the dough and leave it to rise.

Meanwhile soak the apricots and then drain and chop them. Mix with the sugar. Roll out the dough into a rectangle and spread the apricot mixture over it. Roll it up and form it into a ring, with the seam underneath. Place on a greased baking sheet and, with scissors, snip the outside edge of the ring at 2-in (5-cm) intervals. Brush the top with melted butter and scatter over the flaked almonds, pressing a few into the slits. Leave to prove again for 15 minutes.

Preheat the oven to gas mark 6, 400° F, 200° C and bake the ring for 15 minutes. Then turn the oven down to gas mark 5, 375° F, 190° C, and continue cooking for another 10 minutes, or until the ring is cooked. (It will sound hollow if tapped on the bottom.)

Leave to cool on a wire tray and, when the ring is cold, drizzle some white icing over it.

❄ Iced Almond Fingers ❄ (d)

$\frac{1}{2}$ *recipe sweet dough (as in Nut Bread, see p. 140)*
4 oz (125 g) ground almonds
2 oz (50 g) caster sugar
1 egg white

For decoration
white icing

Make the dough and leave it to rise.

For the filling, mix the ground almonds with the sugar and egg white and roll this paste into thin sausage shapes about 3 in ($7\frac{1}{2}$ cm) long.

Roll the dough out and cut into strips about 6 in (15 cm) long and $\frac{3}{4}$ in (2 cm) wide. Take a strip of dough and roll it carefully round each piece of almond paste, making sure that the ends are sealed with the dough. Place the almond fingers on a greased baking sheet and leave to prove for another 15 minutes.

Preheat the oven to gas mark 6, 400° F, 200° C and bake the rolls for about 10 minutes. Cover with foil if they are getting brown and continue baking at gas mark 5, 375° F, 190° C for a further 15 minutes.

Remove from the oven, leave to cool and brush with white icing.

❊ **Walnut Loaf** ❊ (d)

6 oz (175 g) butter
6 oz (175 g) caster sugar
3 eggs
8 oz (230 g) self-raising flour
4 oz (115 g) walnuts, chopped

Cream the butter and the sugar and stir in the beaten eggs. Fold in the flour and add the chopped nuts. Pour into a greased and lined 1-lb (450-g) loaf tin and bake at gas mark 4, 350° F, 180° C for about 1 hour.

This loaf can either be served as a cake, or sliced and buttered.

❊ **Orange Loaf or Buns** ❊ (d)

3 oz (75 g) butter
10 oz (275 g) self-raising flour
4 oz (115 g) caster sugar
grated rind and juice of 1 orange
1 egg
1 dsp jelly marmalade
1 dsp golden syrup or honey
2½ fl oz (75 ml) milk

Rub the butter into the flour and add the sugar and grated orange rind. Beat the egg with the marmalade and golden syrup and stir this into the dry ingredients. Add the orange juice and the milk and then pour the mixture into a greased and lined 1-lb (450-g) loaf tin or bun tins. Bake at about gas mark 4, 350° F, 180° C for 45 minutes. For buns the cooking time will be about 20 minutes. The loaf will be very crumbly but is delicious buttered hot, straight from the oven.

This amount makes about 18 buns.

❄ Date Bread ❄ (d)

> *8 oz (230 g) dried dates, chopped*
> *½ tsp bicarbonate of soda*
> *¼ pt (150 ml) boiling water*
> *1 egg*
> *2 oz (50 g) vanilla sugar (see Lockshen Pudding, p. 107)*
> *½ oz (15 g) butter*
> *5 oz (150 g) self-raising flour*

Mix the dates with the bicarbonate of soda and boiling water and leave for about 5 minutes while you prepare the rest of the cake.

Grease and line a 1-lb (450-g) loaf tin and preheat the oven to gas mark 3, 325° F, 160° C. Mix the egg, sugar, butter and flour and then add the date mixture. Stir very well and pour into the greased loaf tin. Bake for about an hour or until a cocktail stick inserted in the centre comes out clean.

Leave to cool. Serve thinly sliced with fresh butter.

11. Passover Cooking

Traditional food at Passover centres around matzah and the meal made from it, with nuts, eggs and sugar forming the basis of most of the cakes and biscuits, as no flour may be used during the festival. To balance this rather sweet and heavy diet it is a good idea to serve plenty of fruit and vegetable dishes, grilled and roasted meat and light soufflés and creams. At the end of this section is a list of other recipes suitable for Passover, but special care has to be taken to ensure that every ingredient, apart from fresh produce, is kosher for Passover (see Jewish Laws and Festivals, p. 18).

The Seder Meal

Charoset

SAVOURY
Knaidlach (p)
Matzo Kleis Balls for Soup (m)
Tongue and Asparagus Rolls (m)
Halibut in Egg and Lemon Sauce (p)
Salmon Mayonnaise (p)
Courgettes in Fresh Tomato Sauce (p)
Aubergine Diamonds (p)
Cream of Artichoke Soup (d)
Aubergines with Cheese (d)

SWEET
Almond Sponge (p)
Apple Meringue Sponge (p)
Hot Chocolate Soufflé (p)
Scudalini (p)

Hazelnut Sponge Cake with Jemma Filling (p)
Cinnamon Balls (p)
Coconut Pyramids (p)
Almond Petits Fours (p)
Praline Creams (d)
Five-minute Chocolate Pots (d)
Custard Filling (d)

PASSOVER SNACKS
Matzo Brei (d)
Fried Matzo (d)

Other Recipes Suitable for Passover

❊ The Seder Meal ❊

The Festival of Passover begins with the Seder service which is partly a ceremony and partly a meal. Although primarily a family occasion, we always include guests—especially those who are away from home or don't have family of their own. Everyone joins together to re-tell the Exodus story. This is followed by a festive meal and ends with singing. On the table for the Seder service are:

3 matzot, which are symbolic of the unleavened dough the Israelites baked before their escape from the Pharaohs and also represent the poverty they suffered both in Egypt and in the desert

a roasted shankbone, to commemorate the paschal sacrifice which every family brought to the Temple in ancient times

a roasted egg, symbolic of the festival sacrifice which was always additional to the paschal lamb

bitter herbs: horseradish or lettuce are usually used as symbolic of the bitterness of the lives of the slaves in Egypt

charoset: a mixture of nuts, apples, cinnamon and wine symbolic of the 'mortar' used by the Israelites in building treasure cities in Egypt

green herbs: parsley and watercress represent the coming of
    spring and renewed life and hope, but they are dipped in
    salt water to remind us of the tears of the Israelites in Egypt
wine: four cups of wine are drunk during the evening and a
    special extra cup is placed on the table for the prophet Elijah
    who symbolically enters every Jewish home at Passover.

❖ Charoset ❖

There are many versions of this fruit 'mortar' and the ingredients vary considerably. For example, the Israeli one contains bananas, dates and peanuts, while the Yemenite mixture
has spices and figs. The consistency should be that of a paste,
but many people prefer not to grind the nuts and chop them
finely instead, as this gives a crunchy taste. If you are not having
a Seder service, try the charoset on matzo crackers.

1 large cooking apple
3 oz (75 g) almonds, blanched and skinned
2 tsps cinnamon
2 tbsps kosher sweet red wine

Chop the apple and the almonds very finely and sprinkle the
cinnamon over them. Mix to a paste with the wine.

SAVOURY

❖ Knaidlach ❖ (p)

There are two types of Passover dumpling for chicken soup.
One, knaidlach, uses just matzo meal and the other, matzo
kleis, uses whole matzot. The secret of making them light is to
make both mixtures soft and not to keep adding matzo meal
when handling them. Chilling the mixture before forming them
into balls also helps.

6 oz (175 g) matzo meal, medium-ground
¼ pt (150 ml) water
1 tsp salt
pinch ginger
3 eggs
6 tbsps oil

Mix the matzo meal with the water and seasoning. Then add
the well-beaten eggs and oil and form the mixture into small
balls (about ¾-in (2-cm) diameter). Chill the knaidlach for a few
hours and then cook them in boiling water for about 20 minutes.
They will rise to the surface and double in size. Drain them and
serve in hot chicken soup.

This amount makes about 36 small balls.

❋ Matzo Kleis Balls for Soup ❋   (m)

2 matzot
1 onion, chopped and fried in 2 tbsps chicken fat
1 tbsp parsley, chopped
2 eggs
salt, pepper
2–4 tbsps matzo meal, medium-ground
pinch ginger

Soak the matzot in cold water for about 5 minutes and then
drain and squeeze them dry. Mash them with a fork and mix in
the chopped, fried onion and parsley. Stir in the beaten eggs,
season with salt, pepper and ginger and add about 1 tablespoon
matzo meal. Dip your hands in matzo meal and roll the mixture
into small balls about 1-in (2½-cm) diameter. Chill the balls and
then drop them into fast-boiling soup and cook for about 20
minutes.

❋ Tongue and Asparagus Rolls ❋   (m)

For this dish you can either use slices of ready-cooked tongue or prepare your own. A whole tongue is very good for a buffet table and the slices may be used in many ways. This one makes an attractive starter.

1 3–4-lb (1½–1¾-kg) pickled beef tongue
1 onion
1 carrot
1 bay leaf
6 peppercorns
8 oz (225 g) asparagus tips, cooked

Soak the tongue in cold water for a few hours before cooking. Place it in a deep saucepan with fresh water, together with the onion, carrot, bay leaf and peppercorns. Bring to the boil, skim, then simmer, covered, for about 3 hours or until the tongue is tender. Remove it from the pan and while it is still hot, take off the thick skin and any membranes and then curl it into a 6-in (15-cm) round tin or container. Cover with a small plate and place a weight on top. Leave in the refrigerator after it has cooled and, when it is quite cold, cut it into thin round slices.

Roll the slices of tongue round one or two asparagus tips and shape into cornets. Arrange these round a dish and serve cold with salads.

✤ Halibut in Egg and Lemon Sauce ✤ (p)

A traditional Passover cold dish with a light and delicious (non-fattening) lemon sauce, which keeps well in the refrigerator.

1 small onion
½ pt (¼ l) water
1 tsp sugar
salt, pepper
4 halibut steaks
3–4 egg yolks
juice of 2 lemons (reserve a few slices for decoration)

Slice the onion into a large shallow pan, cover with the water and seasoning and bring to the boil. Simmer for about 10 minutes and then carefully lower in the halibut steaks. Cook over a low heat for about 10 minutes and then remove the fish with a slotted spoon to a serving dish. Reduce the cooking liquid over high heat for a few minutes.

Beat the egg yolks with the lemon juice and pour on the strained fish liquid. Return the sauce to the pan and stir carefully over a very low heat, taking great care not to let it boil. When the sauce thickens remove it immediately and pour it over the fish. Leave to cool and garnish with slices of fresh lemon.

❄ Salmon Mayonnaise ❄   (p)

This is a good way to cook salmon when it is to be served cold as it preserves all the juices and leaves the fish moist and succulent. It can be prepared the day before.

> *1 5–6-lb (2–3-kg) whole salmon*
> *1 lemon*
> *salt, pepper*
> *2 tbsps oil*

> For the mayonnaise
> *1 whole egg*
> *1 egg yolk*
> *½ tsp sugar*
> *salt, pepper*
> *2 tbsps vinegar or lemon juice*
> *½ pt (¼ l) oil*

Place the fish in the centre of an oiled piece of tin foil. Put a few slices of lemon inside the fish and put the rest on top with the seasoning. Sprinkle with oil and wrap up the foil to make a loose parcel.

Cook the salmon in a preheated oven (gas mark 7, 425° F,

220° C) for about 15 minutes and then turn the oven off. (A larger fish may take about 30 minutes.) Leave the salmon in the foil parcel in the oven until it is cold, when it will be just cooked and none of the juices will be lost.

For the mayonnaise, mix together the egg, egg yolk, seasoning and vinegar or lemon juice and then very gradually add the oil, drop by drop, until the mayonnaise is thick and pale. (This can be done in a blender, in which case you pour the oil in very slowly in a steady stream.)

❈ Courgettes in Fresh Tomato Sauce ❈   (p)

1 lb (450 g) courgettes
½ lb (225 g) onions, chopped
1 tbsp oil
1 lb (450 g) tomatoes, peeled and chopped
1 tsp sugar
salt, pepper

Cut the courgettes into slices or strips and cook in very little salted water for about 7 minutes.

Sauté the onion in oil and stir until it is slightly golden. Add the tomatoes, sugar, salt and pepper and cook over low heat for about 15 minutes.

Put the drained courgettes in a serving dish and sieve the tomato sauce over the top. Serve cold as a starter or a side dish with cold meat or fish, or hot as a vegetable.

❈ Aubergine Diamonds ❈   (p)

4 aubergines (about 1¾ lb (800 g))
2 large onions, chopped
olive oil for frying
4 large eggs
salt, pepper
dash lemon juice

Cook the aubergines at gas mark 7, 425° F, 220° C for about 40 minutes or until they are soft. Cut them in half and scrape the flesh off the skins. Sauté the onion in the oil and add this to the aubergine, mashing them well together. Beat the eggs with the seasoning and lemon juice and stir into the aubergine mixture. Pour it into a greased baking dish and cook at gas mark 6, 400° F, 200° C for about 30 minutes when it will be crisp at the edges.

Cut into diamond shapes and serve hot or cold.

❊ Cream of Artichoke Soup ❊ (d)

This soup is a good choice for Passover because the artichokes which give it its characteristic taste are in season in the early spring and also no thickening is needed.

> 2 tbsps butter
> ¼ lb (125 g) small mushrooms, sliced
> 2 onions, chopped
> 1 lb (450 g) Jerusalem artichokes, peeled and sliced
> ½ pt (¼ l) vegetable stock (see Potato Soup, p. 41)
> ½ pt (¼ l) milk
> salt, pepper

> For decoration
> parsley, chopped

Melt the butter in a saucepan and sauté the mushrooms for 1 minute. Put them on a plate and then sauté the onions and artichokes. (Add a little more butter if necessary.) Do not let the vegetables brown and when they start to soften add the stock. Bring to the boil and simmer until the artichokes are cooked. Then either sieve or blend the soup to make a thick purée. Heat the milk in the saucepan, stir in the purée and add the sliced mushrooms. Season to taste. Reheat gently and serve with a little chopped parsley.

❖ Aubergines with Cheese ❖   (d)

> 2 large aubergines
> 1 onion, chopped
> oil for frying
> 1 lb (450 g) fresh tomatoes, peeled and sliced
> 6 oz (175 g) Dutch cheese thinly sliced
> salt, pepper

Slice the aubergines, cover them with salt and leave in a colander for 30 minutes to remove the bitter juices. Wash and drain the slices and then sauté them in the oil with the chopped onion. In a casserole, put in a layer of aubergine slices, some of the onion and cover with the tomato slices and cheese. Continue until all the ingredients are used up, finishing with a layer of cheese. Season well and cook at gas mark 6, 400° F, 200° C for about 40 minutes, when the cheese will be bubbling and brown.

SWEET

❖ Almond Sponge ❖   (p)

> 6 large eggs, separated
> 8 oz (225 g) caster sugar
> 8 oz (225 g) ground almonds
> 1 tbsp matzo meal, fine-ground

Whisk the egg yolks with the sugar until they are pale and thick. This will take about 5 minutes with an electric mixer or about 20 minutes by hand. Then gently fold in the ground almonds, the stiffly whisked egg whites and the matzo meal. Spoon the mixture into a 10-in (25-cm) cake tin (or 2 sandwich tins) and bake in a preheated oven (gas mark 4, 350° F, 180° C) for about 30 minutes. Test to see if the centre is cooked.

Serve either hot as a pudding or cold as a cake.

❖ Apple Meringue Sponge ❖   (p)

>   1 6–8-in (15–20-cm) almond sponge cake (half quantity for
>   previous recipe)
>   2 lb (900 g) cooking apples, peeled and sliced
>   4 oz (125 g) caster sugar
>   2 egg whites

Make the sponge cake as in the previous recipe and place it in
an ovenproof dish of the same size as the tin in which the cake
was baked. Cook the apples over low heat with very little water
and about 2 tablespoons of sugar. When they are soft, mash them
and spoon the mixture over the almond cake.

Whisk the egg whites until they are stiff and then add the
remaining sugar until the meringue is very firm. Pipe or spread
it over the apple mixture, making sure that the whole cake is
completely covered. Bake at gas mark 4, 350° F, 180° C for
about 25 minutes, when the top will be golden-brown but the
meringue will be soft inside. Serve either hot or cold.

❖ Hot Chocolate Soufflé ❖   (p)

The word 'soufflé' might make you think this is difficult. It is
really just a cooked chocolate mousse and is ideal for a special
occasion, any time of the year, but is especially suitable for
Passover as it contains no flour. There will be enough for
about 5 people—some may prefer the centre which will be
thick and runny, while the sides should be just set.

>   7 oz (200 g) chocolate
>   4 egg yolks
>   6 egg whites
>   3 oz (75 g) caster sugar

Grease an 8-in (20-cm) soufflé dish and sprinkle the base and
sides with a little sugar. Preheat the oven to gas mark 5, 375° F,
190° C.

Melt the chocolate in a pan over simmering water and then mix it with the beaten egg yolks. Whisk the whites and gradually add the sugar until they are very stiff. Fold the whites into the chocolate and carefully spoon the soufflé into the dish.

Cook for about 25 minutes and serve immediately.

❊ Scudalini ❊ (p)

A very rich Portuguese and Gibraltarian dessert, generally served in tiny pots. Don't be put off by the number of egg yolks in the recipe—it makes about 12 portions and keeps well.

> *4 oz (125 g) caster sugar*
> *¼ pt (150 ml) water*
> *1 vanilla pod*
> *12 egg yolks*
> *1 tsp cinnamon*

Make a syrup with the sugar, water and vanilla pod (see Queijinhos, p. 124) and when it is thick remove it from the heat and pour it slowly on to the beaten egg yolks, stirring all the time. Cook the mixture, in a double saucepan, until it starts to thicken, and then pour it into small pots. When it is cold sprinkle over a little cinnamon and keep refrigerated until ready to serve.

❊ Hazelnut Sponge Cake with Jemma Filling ❊ (p)

A traditional Sephardi cake with the rich jemma (egg and sugar) filling.

> For the cake
> *6 eggs, separated*
> *6 oz (175 g) caster sugar*
> *grated rind and juice of 1 lemon*
> *6 oz (175 g) hazelnuts, ground*
> *1 oz (25 g) matzo meal, fine-ground*

For the filling
6 egg yolks
4 oz (125 g) caster sugar
2½ fl oz (75 ml) water
1 vanilla pod

First make the jemma filling (see Qeuijinhos, p. 124).

Whisk the egg yolks and sugar and add the grated rind and juice of the lemon. Add the dry ingredients and bake as for Almond Sponge (see p. 153) for 30 to 40 minutes.

Leave the cakes to cool on a wire tray and then sandwich them together with the cooled jemma. Dust the top with icing sugar.

❖ Cinnamon Balls ❖ (p)

2 egg whites
6 oz (175 g) ground almonds
3 oz (75 g) caster sugar
1 tbsp cinnamon
icing sugar

Whisk the egg whites until they are stiff and then add the ground almonds, sugar and cinnamon. Roll into small balls and bake on a greased tray at gas mark 4, 350° F, 180° C for about 25 minutes. They should be slightly soft inside—too much cooking will make them hard and tough. Cool them for about 5 minutes and then roll in sifted icing sugar.

❖ Coconut Pyramids ❖ (p)

8 oz (225 g) desiccated coconut
4 oz (125 g) caster sugar
2 eggs (or just the whites)

Mix all the ingredients together and form into small pyramids by hand, dipping your fingers in cold water to prevent the mixture from sticking. Place the biscuits on a greased tin and bake at gas mark 5, 375° F, 190° C for about 15 minutes. They will be quite soft and the tips just beginning to turn golden.

❊ Almond Petits Fours ❊ (p)

1–2 egg whites
7 oz (200 g) ground almonds
7 oz (200 g) icing sugar

Whisk the egg whites until they are stiff. Stir the ground almonds into the icing sugar and pour in enough of the beaten egg whites to form a firm mixture. (If it is too soft the biscuits will lose their shape.) With a forcing bag, pipe out small rosettes on to a greased tin and bake at gas mark 7, 425° F, 220° C for about 10 minutes. Take the petits fours out of the oven, remove carefully from the tin as they will still seem quite soft, and leave to cool and harden slightly on a wire tray.

❊ Praline Creams ❊ (d)

4 oz (125 g) unsalted butter
4 oz (125 g) caster sugar
2 eggs, separated
¼ pt (150 ml) milk
4 oz (125 g) ground almonds

For the praline
2 oz (50 g) almonds, flaked
3 oz (75 g) caster sugar

Beat the butter until it is soft and then add 2 oz (50 g) sugar, and continue beating until the mixture is soft and fluffy.

Mix the egg yolks with the milk and the rest of the sugar and stir over very low heat until the mixture thickens slightly, taking great care not to let it curdle. Leave this custard to cool and then fold it into the butter mixture with the ground almonds.

Whisk the egg whites until they are stiff and fold these in too. Pour the mixture into small pots.

For the praline, put the almonds and sugar in a small heavy pan and heat very slowly. When the sugar starts to melt it will gradually turn from a thick white mixture to a transparent golden caramel. When it is brown, turn it out immediately on to an oiled surface (or foil) and spread it out. It will cool quickly and the nuts will be toasted and brown. Chop it roughly with a rolling pin and sprinkle it over the almond creams. (The praline keeps well in an airtight container and can also be used in ice creams and cakes.)

Variation: for chocolate creams, add ¼ lb (125 g) melted chocolate to the custard.

❋ Five-minute Chocolate Pots ❋ (d)

7½ fl oz (225 ml) milk
½ lb (225 g) chocolate, grated or broken into pieces
4 egg yolks

Heat the milk in a saucepan and add the chocolate. When it has melted bring the chocolate milk to the boil and then pour it on to the beaten egg yolks. Whisk until smooth and then strain the cream into small cups and chill for a few hours. Serve very cold.

❋ Custard Filling ❋ (d)

This Passover custard is good as a cake filling, served with cooked fruit or used as the basis of ice cream.

For the custard
2 eggs
2 oz (50 g) vanilla sugar (see Lockshen Pudding, p. 107)
1 tsp potato flour
½ pt (¼ l) milk

For ice cream
2 egg whites
½ pt (¼ l) fruit purée or mashed bananas

Mix the eggs, sugar and potato flour together and stir in the warmed milk. Return the mixture to the saucepan and stir carefully over low heat until the custard is thick, taking great care not to let it boil.

To make the ice cream, whisk the egg whites until stiff and then fold in the cooled custard and puréed or mashed fruit. Freeze for about 1 hour, whisk again and then freeze until firm.

PASSOVER SNACKS

After several heavy festive meals, here are two ideas for a savoury or sweet snack. They are both easy, quick and cheap and should be served and eaten straight from the pan.

❋ Matzo Brei ❋   (d)

For each person you need:
2 matzot
2 eggs
salt, pepper
1 tbsp butter

Soak the matzot for a few minutes in boiling water and then squeeze them dry. Beat them with a fork and then add the beaten eggs and seasoning. Fry in hot butter, stirring gently until just set—like scrambled eggs.

❋ Fried Matzo ❋   (d)

For each person you need:
1 egg
1 tbsp milk
1 matzo, quartered or 3–4 matzo crackers

For the topping
*1 tbsp sugar, flavoured with a good pinch of cinnamon or 1 tbsp
    grated cheese and a sliced tomato*

Beat the egg and milk together and soak the matzo or crackers in it while you prepare the sweet or savoury topping.

Drain the matzo and then fry in hot butter for a few minutes on both sides. Transfer to heated plates and either toss in cinnamon sugar or cover with grated cheese and a sliced tomato.

❈ Other Recipes Suitable for Passover ❈

STARTERS AND SIDE DISHES

Fried Chicken Pick-ups (p. 27) (m)
Chopped Liver (p. 28) (m)
Avocados with Chicken Salad (p. 29) (m)
Chicken Soup (p. 37) (m)
Frankfurters and Potato Salad (p. 92) (m)
Potato Latkes (p. 63) (p)
Red Pepper Salad (p. 94) (p)
Pink Grapefruit Cocktail (p. 31) (p)
Melon with Orange Jelly (p. 32) (p)
Potato Soup (p. 41) (d)
Chilled Beetroot Borscht (p. 43) (d)

MAIN COURSES

Spanish Chicken (p. 82) (m)
Braised Chicken with Onions (p. 83) (m)
Chicken with Aubergines (p. 84) (m)
Duck with Apples and Honey (p. 85) (m)
Veal in White Onion Sauce (p. 81) (m)
Turkey Schnitzels with Lemon (p. 86) (m)
Fried Fish (p. 46) (p)
Gefilte Fish Balls (p. 46) (p)
Baked Trout (p. 49) (p)

DESSERTS

Lemon Mousse (p. 104) (p)
Chocolate Mousse (p. 105) (p)
Queijinhos (p. 124) (p)
Iced Apricot Mousse (p. 108) (d)

Index

Index